The
· Transport ·
Treasury

Old Oak Common
Andrew Wilson

The Transport Treasury

Reviving the memories of yesterday…

© Images and design: The Transport Treasury 2022. Text Andrew Wilson.

ISBN 978-1-913251-40-6

First published in 2022 by Transport Treasury Publishing Ltd., 16 Highworth Close, High Wycombe, HP13 7PJ

www.ttpublishing.co.uk

Printed in Tarxien, Malta by Gutenberg Press Ltd.

**The copyright holders hereby give notice that all rights to this work are reserved.
Aside from brief passages for the purpose of review, no part of this work may be reproduced, copied by electronic or other means, or otherwise stored in any information storage and retrieval system without written permission from the Publisher. This includes the illustrations herein which shall remain the copyright of the copyright holder.**

Front Cover: Dick Riley photographed immaculately turned out Castle Class 4-6-0 No 5066 *Sir Felix Pole* outside one of the two entrances to Old Oak Common's south-east turntables on 20 May 1956. Until 1938 these entrances were single but to ease movements were doubled. No 5066 had entered Swindon Works at the end of March for an unclassified repair prior to being renamed *Sir Felix Pole*, to commemorate the GWR's most influential and dynamic General Manager who was in office between 1921 and 1929. When completed in July 1937 No 5066 was named *Wardour Castle* and entered traffic from Old Oak Common on 16 July. It unusually remained allocated to Old Oak Common until withdrawn from traffic on 17th September 1962. Before this occurred it was fitted with a four-row superheater boiler and double chimney in April 1959 and when withdrawn was coupled to Hawksworth flat-sided tender No 4060. *RCR7280*

Frontispiece: Despite being only five months away from closing to steam, Dick Riley captured an image of some of Old Oak Common's remaining tired and neglected pannier tanks alongside the coal on 12th September 1964, which gave lie to the shed's imminent demise despite a Western Class C-C diesel-hydraulic stabled in the distance. At the head of the row of three 9400 and three 8750 Class 0-6-0PTs is No 9435, new in January 1951 and first allocated to Wolverhampton Stafford Road. Only transferred to Old Oak Common in July 1963, No 9435 would be withdrawn by the end of September. By this time the pannier tanks were restricted to stock movements in and out of Paddington as well as shed pilot turns. Only the right hand road of the coal stage has wagons awaiting unloading as the shed's principal passenger turns were now in the hands of diesel traction. *RCR17722*

Westbury allocated Hawksworth Modified Hall Class 4-6-0 No 7917 *North Aston Hall* has its tender topped up with some choice lumps of Welsh steam coal on 21st September 1958. Hand coaling at this date was anachronistic on all regions other than the Western but as Welsh steam coal was soft and friable there was really no alternative. One of the hand filled coal tubs is in the process of emptying its contents into No 7917's tender. The only concession to protecting the coalmen from the elements were the canopies, but with a southerly or south-westerly wind blowing they offered little if any shelter. No 7917 was completed at Swindon in May 1950 and so never carried GWR livery, instead it was outshopped in BR mixed traffic black. Happily, by the time Dick Riley captured it on film it was carrying fully lined out green. Withdrawal from Oxford shed came during the first week of August 1965. *RCR12769*

Rear Cover: Churchward's 4700 Class of mixed traffic 2-8-0s may have been only a small class of nine locomotives but they were undoubtedly the pride of Old Oak Common's eight-coupled locomotives and when time was found to clean them thoroughly they made a magnificent sight. When in this condition they were the one class that could eclipse the shed's 'Kings' and 'Castles' in appearance. Seen on 27th October 1957, No 4704 had been specially cleaned for the visit of Dick Riley and the crew happily moved it around the shed and carriage sidings for the photographer. In this view No 4704 is outside the straight shed built to service Old Oak Common's diesel railcars and multiple units. No 4704 was the second of the class to receive fully lined out passenger green and had entered traffic in April 1922 and was withdrawn in May 1964. *RCR11382*

Contents

Old Oak Common: BR Steam 1948-1965 - Andrew Wilson

Introduction

Old Oak Common: those three words immediately transport me back to the late 1950s and early 1960s when G. J. Churchward's magnificent cathedral of Great Western steam witnessed the transition from steam to diesel traction. The engine shed could so easily have been called Wormwood Scrubs, Scrubs Lane or Mitre Bridge, but somehow none of these would have conjured up the same images of the GWR's principal London shed. Old Oak Common's raison d'être was to provide locomotives for Paddington's passenger services to the Midlands, South Wales, Bristol, Shrewsbury and Birkenhead as well as the SouthWest of England. There were also the important parcels, express goods and postal services, the local trip workings, shunters, and sufficient motive power for the carriage stock movements into and out of the terminus. So, it was not surprising that on 1st January 1948 the shed's allocation included 89 4-6-0s and 89 tank engines.

Old Oak Common was a relatively young locomotive depot, having opened on 17th March 1906 when it replaced the inadequate and constricted shed at Westbourne Park, which in turn had replaced the early broad gauge shed at Westbourne Terrace. The rapid expansion of domestic housing towards the end of the 19th century in London caused the Great Western to look west for a site suitable for a large, well laid out shed, repair shop, carriage shed and sidings. A triangular plot of 78acres of rough grazing three miles west of Paddington abutting the Grand Union Canal was chosen which was part of Old Oak Farm and known locally as Old Oak Common. The almost triangular piece of land was bounded in the east close to where the West London Junction Railway crossed the GWR main line and Grand Junction (Paddington Branch) Canal, later the Grand Union Canal, at Mitre Bridge on the northern edge of Wormwood Scrubs. The western boundary was effectively where the Hampstead Junction Railway ran and was later delineated by Old Oak Common Lane. However, the site would need levelling, as the western boundary was some 15ft higher than the eastern.

Planning began during the latter part of William Dean's tenure at Swindon when his faculties were waning and so the influential hand of George Jackson Churchward can be seen behind the development. Not only was the shed to become the largest on the GWR, but it would also be the prototype of the internal turntable depot. The concept of the shed was in advance of its contemporaries, being capable of handling much larger locomotives than were in service at the time and using electricity from the outset.

The Architects Department at Swindon Works surveyed the site and drew up the drawings and specifications for submission to the GWR Board. After the plans had been signed off the Company was in a position to request tenders for the building works early in 1902. An early tender costed the work at £70,000 while in July another priced the work at £110,000. After the receipt of further tenders, one for £40,313 was accepted in December 1902 with an additional one in April 1905 of £2,500 for extra works. As was the usual practice the work was subcontracted by the main contractor Messrs Walkerdine of Derby who worked under the supervision of the GWR's New Works Engineer, W. Armstrong, who in turn was answerable to F. W. Wright, Churchward's deputy.

The layout was designed to ensure there were as few conflicting movements as possible between locomotives going off shed and those coming in for servicing. The main shed contained four boarded over 65ft undergirder turntables, each driven by an electric tractor. All were interconnected as well as having individual access roads, the two at the back through sidewalls and those at the front through the end gable wall. The 360ft by 444ft shed was constructed of red brick, embellished with roundnosed blue engineers' bricks and roofed in slate. The trussed roof was supported by 60ft steel girders. The one hundred stabling roads each had individual smokehoods that vented through a series of longitudinal louvres.

The coal stage incorporated four double and two single chutes, which allowed two or three locomotives to be coaled simultaneously from each side. The south side was supplied with the best quality Welsh steam coal for passenger locomotives and the north side with inferior grades of coal suitable for freight classes and tank engines. To allow this separation of coal grades there were two coal roads into the stage accessed by a 1 in 50 gradient. These sidings continued for 100yds beyond the stage on a reduced 1 in 80 incline. Due to the soft nature of Welsh steam coal the GWR was never able to use cenotaph mechanical coal towers. The water tank over the stage had a capacity of 290,000 gallons and was effectively four standard tanks joined together. At ground level were the mess rooms for the coalmen.

The GWR coded Old Oak Common as 'PDN' but 'OOC' was also used, either being stencilled on the leading edge of the footplate valance. After Nationalisation as the main shed in the No.1 District, London, it was coded as 81A with shedplates bolted to the bottom part of the smokebox doors. As the premier GWR shed it was invariably allocated the latest classes and so 'Castles' and 'Kings' replaced 'Stars' and 'Saints' while 'Halls' brought about the demise of the Churchward 4-4-0s. This also applied to the 0-6-0PTs where the '5700' class replaced the Armstrong and Dean tank engines only to be in their turn superseded by the later '8750' and '9400' classes. Not all new designs enjoyed long stays at 81A as both the 'County' 4-6-0s and 'Britannia' 4-6-2s allocations were moved away as quickly as possible.

With the gradual introduction of diesel hydraulic traction to the Western Region from 1958 onwards Old Oak Common's allocation of steam locomotives began to be reduced. In 1964 work began on demolishing the main shed to provide accommodation for the servicing of diesel locomotives and diesel multiple units. In March 1965, almost 59 years to the day after it opened, Old Oak Common was closed to steam. Those locomotives not withdrawn were in the main transferred to Southall and by 27th March the shed was a diesel depot. The last classes to depart were all '8750' and '9400' pannier tanks.

Andrew Wilson, May 2022

This 1953 plan of Old Oak Common illustrates the layout after the access lines to the roundhouses had been doubled. As far as possible the repair shop and its associated sidings are separated from the day-to-day running of the shed. Engines arriving on shed would have their ash pans and smokeboxes cleaned before being coaled and water would be taken on as necessary before being stabled either in the roundhouses or, if a quick turnaround was needed, on one of the sidings. Sunday mornings would usually see the shed full.

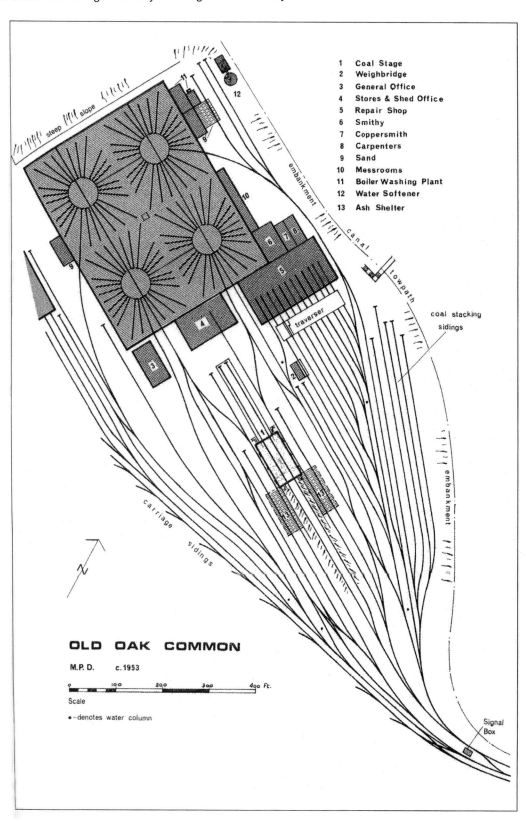

1   Coal Stage
2   Weighbridge
3   General Office
4   Stores & Shed Office
5   Repair Shop
6   Smithy
7   Coppersmith
8   Carpenters
9   Sand
10 Messrooms
11 Boiler Washing Plant
12 Water Softener
13 Ash Shelter

OLD OAK COMMON

M.P.D.   c.1953

0   100   200   300   400 Ft.
Scale

•—denotes water column

Chapter 1
Old Oak's Principal Allocations

The 'Kings' were both the GWR and Western Region's flagship passenger class and from their introduction at the end of June 1927 until January 1963 Old Oak Common was never without an allocation. On 20th May 1956, No 6002 *King Edward IV* stands outside the original entrance to the southeast section of the main shed building in its final form. Rebuilt with a double blast pipe and chimney the locomotive also carries the final development of the 'King' boiler classified WB with its large superheater cover on the smokebox and mechanical lubricator ahead of the driver's side outside steam pipe. New to traffic in July 1927, No 6001 was allocated to Laira, Newton Abbot or Exeter until moved to Stafford Road in December 1948. In July 1950, it was transferred to Old Oak Common but returned to Laira in June 1959 only to move back to West London in September 1960. A final transfer to Stafford Road came in June 1962 before withdrawal the following September. *RCR7282*

Numerically the 'Castles' were Old Oak Common's largest class of passenger locomotives with around 30 on the books before dieselisation began to make them redundant. On 12th October 1957, the recently ex-works No 5065 *Newport Castle* makes a magnificent sight as the winter sun sinks in the western sky. To traffic in July 1937 when named *Upton Castle*, it was renamed in September 1937. Originally allocated to Exeter it became a Cardiff Canton member of the class in August 1939 until December 1944 when it was transferred to Old Oak Common from where it was condemned in January 1963. Coupled to Hawksworth flatsided tender No 4076, which gave a more modern appearance, No 5065 received its last Heavy General overhaul in December 1960 and ended its working life coupled to Hawksworth tender No 4039. *RCR11332*

There was almost parity between the number of 'Castles' and 'Halls' allocated to Old Oak Common until the shed's final rundown and closure to steam. On 23rd September 1956, the doyen of the 330-strong class No 4900 *Saint Martin* carrying British Railways lined-black mixed-traffic livery looks well used but reasonably clean. When Collett rebuilt 'Saint' class 4-6-0 No 2925 *Saint Martin* in December 1925 with 6ft coupled wheels, few would have thought that the locomotive would be the precursor of the LMS 'Black Five', the LNER 'B1' and British Railways Riddles '5MT' 4-6-0s, a total of 1,424 locomotives in addition to a further 329 'Halls'. No 4900 was allocated to Old Oak Common on six occasions in GWR days but only once after Nationalisation, from October 1956 until withdrawal at the beginning of April 1959. *RCR8004*

Above: The Hawksworth 'Modified Halls' featured a number of changes from the Collett 'Halls' including a plate frame bogie, altered springing, lengthened wheelbase, modified front frames and larger three row superheaters in addition to being coupled to the new flatsided tenders. Released to traffic at the end of November 1947, No 6978 *Haroldstone Hall* is pictured at Old Oak Common on 27th October 1957, less than two months after receiving a Heavy Casual repair at Swindon. First allocated to 81A in January 1957, No 6978 was not transferred away until the end of February 1965 when moved to Severn Tunnel Junction. The stencilled 'ID' on the front valance behind the buffer beam indicates that it has been given improved draughting and so permitted to take heavier loads than unaltered members of the class. This proved invaluable to shed masters at busy periods when traffic was heavy as a freshly shopped engine could be substituted for a 'Castle'. *RCR11376*

Opposite Top: Churchward's last new class for the GWR was the magnificent and highly regarded mixed traffic '4700' 2-8-0s that were associated with Old Oak Common from 1919 until 1964. The '4700s' were a logical development of the versatile '4300' class 2-6-0s and the 5ft 8in 2-8-0s carried the large Standard No 7 boiler. The nine strong class was the first to be given outside steam pipes; a feature that became standard, and usually 81A had five on its books. On Sunday, 12th August 1956, the shed's No 4701 is stabled at Old Oak Common awaiting its next rostered duty, no doubt an overnight long distance fast fitted freight. No 4701 carries British Railways' first livery for the class, plain black, although later No 4702 was lined out in red, cream and grey. From mid-1957 Swindon turned the class out in lined passenger green, a livery that suited the bulk of the engines better than plain black. *4701*

Opposite Bottom: The Collett '6100' 262Ts were introduced in 1931 to handle the Paddington suburban workings with 70 constructed between April 1931 and November 1935. To improve acceleration the boiler pressure, compared to the '5101' 2-6-2Ts, was raised by 200psi to 225psi. The result was a class that satisfied the demands of the traffic department and Old Oak usually had an allocation of around 15 in the 1950s. Like all the 2-6-2Ts the class was well proportioned as illustrated by No 6135, an Old Oak Common engine throughout the British Railways era, on its home shed on 23rd June 1957. The class was eventually painted green but not all were fully lined out like No 6135. This '6100' entered traffic in October 1932 and was withdrawn in December 1965 from Oxford where it had been transferred in September of that year from Southall after No 6135 moved there in September 1964. *RCR10813*

Above: On 1st January 1948, Old Oak Common had an allocation of 232 locomotives of which 88 were '5700' / '8750' class pannier tanks making them by far the shed's largest single class. Even in 1959 when diesel shunters were allocated to the shed in numbers there were 47 on the books making them still the largest single class, although by this date they were supplemented by 17 of the Hawksworth '9400' 0-6-0PTs. A rather scruffy No 8763 is seen on the ash pits at Old Oak Common on 16th August 1959 still showing signs of the mixed traffic lining applied to it and classmates Nos 8764, 8771 and 8773. The thinking behind this move was that the engines would be kept clean and so make a better impression on the travelling public at Paddington. Unfortunately, as can be seen, this was a forlorn hope as cleaners were few and far between at the shed by this time. *RCR14148*

Opposite Top: Ten pannier tanks, Nos 9701-9710, were built in 1933 with condensing apparatus to replace the ageing '633' 0-6-0Ts and 2-4-0Ts fitted with similar equipment to work over the Metropolitan lines to Smithfield after No 8700 was rebuilt in March 1932. The tanks were shortened at the smokebox and the capacity reduced to 1,080 gallons and a vertical feed pump fitted on the right side. Two branch pipes from the smokebox took the exhaust steam to the tanks, which were fitted with vents. On the production '9700s' the capacity of the tanks was increased to 1,230 gallons by the simple expedient of extending the rear pannier tanks into side tanks. The condensing engines were fitted with modified ATC apparatus which was automatically clipped up clear of the live rail when entering an electrified section and releasing it upon leaving. No 9704 is seen inside Old Oak Common shed on 23 June 1957. *NS200676B*

Opposite Bottom: The Hawksworth '9400' class 0-6-0PTs were a development of the Collett '5700'/'8750' classes fitted with Standard No 10 taper boilers and were introduced in 1947. The first ten, Nos 9400-09, were the only examples built by the GWR and so put into traffic in green with GWR on the side tanks and they were the only members of the class that were superheated. Old Oak Common's No 9402, seen on shed on 12th June 1949, illustrates the main features of the class. Unfortunately the use of the No 10 boiler made the '9400s' heavier than the Collett design and put them into the red route class, thus restricting their use. By 1959 81A had an allocation of 13 and they were used alongside the '5700'/'8750s' on the Paddington empty stock work and general shunting. Five of the class were among the last steam locomotives to depart from 81A in March 1965. *9402*

Chapter 2
The 'Kings'

Above: Sundays in the 1950s usually found Old Oak Common struggling to find enough siding space to accommodate all the locomotives waiting to take up their Sunday night and Monday booked turns and 7th August 1955, was no exception as 'King' class 4-6-0 No 6002 *King William IV* is stabled behind a 'Castle' on the northern side of the shed. A Newton Abbot Division 'King', in GWR days, it was first allocated to Old Oak Common from Wolverhampton Stafford Road in July 1950 before returning to Laira in June 1959. Back at 81A in September 1960 its last move was back to Stafford Road in June 1962. The boiler carried is a GWR design 'WA' distinguishable by the smaller superheater header cover seen here. It would not be until March 1956 that No 6002 was fitted with a double chimney and blastpipe. *ES2693*

Opposite Top: Although all 30 of the 'Kings' were allocated to Old Oak Common, ranging from a few weeks to many decades, only one, No 6009 *King Charles II*, spent its entire working life at the shed. Seen on 7th August 1955, No 6009 looks as if it is still in GWR condition but it actually carries the modified 'WB' boiler and single chimney with the larger diameter outside steam pipes fitted by the Western Region. New to Old Oak Common in April 1928, withdrawal did not come until September 1962. Having been painted blue until March 1953 it now carries passenger green lined out in orange and black. The shovel on the tender was, moments before this fine portrait was taken, being used to level the coal in the tender, perhaps indicative of an imminent departure to Paddington to pick up a down express. *ES2689*

Opposite Bottom: Due to their maximum axle loading of 22½ tons the 'Kings' had limited route availability, shown by the unique use of two red route discs above the cabside numberplates. Nevertheless from their introduction until withdrawal the GWR and the Western Region of British Railways regarded them as their premier passenger class, in fact the only Swindon built '8P'. With their large boilers and wide cylinders they made the most of the GWR's generous loading gauge, making them impressive looking locomotives as illustrated by single chimney No 6018 *King Henry VI*, seen on Old Oak Common shed on 27th October 1957 behind an unidentified '4700' class 2-8-0. No 6018 was first allocated to Old Oak Common in July 1950. In September 1960 it moved to Cardiff Canton but was back in West London in June 1962 until being withdrawn in December of that year. *RCR11378*

Opposite Top: Wolverhampton Stafford Road's 'King' class 4-6-0 No 6020 *King Henry IV* is seen in charge of a 13-coach down express from Paddington to Birmingham and Wolverhampton at Old Oak Common East on 20th August 1955. The train is composed of mainly ex-GWR Hawksworth, Collett and Churchward stock and is overtaking an empty carriage working heading for Old Oak Common's carriage sidings. In the background is Kensal Green Gasworks with its enormous gasholder while behind the empty stock and flyover approach is the wall of the Grand Union Canal. Along with Nos 6006 and 6008 this 'King' was one of the three members of the class to be allocated to Old Oak Common for a matter of weeks rather than years. In GWR days *King Henry IV* was primarily a Newton Abbot Division locomotive and in British Railways days a Wolverhampton Division 'King'. *RCR6552*

Opposite Bottom: There were two failures of 'King' bogies in January 1956 and on 23rd January, 27 were taken out of traffic and their bogies removed for examination leaving only Nos 6000, 6006 and 6022 in traffic. To ease the Western Region's motive power shortage two Stanier Pacifics, Nos 46254 and 46257, were loaned to Old Oak Common. On 4th February, three 'Kings', Nos 6013 *King Henry VIII*, an unidentified member engine and No 6028 *King George VI*, have had their bogies removed and are stored at Old Oak Common. No sooner had the bogies been checked than serious mainframe cracks were discovered, resulting in the whole class being withdrawn for remedial action. Temporary replacements in the form of Stanier Pacifics Nos 46207 and 46210 and eight Standard '5MT' class 4-6-0s were loaned to the Western Region. It was not until the end of February that all the 'Kings' were back in traffic. *RCR5801*

Above: Stafford Road's 'King' No 6011 *King James I* has arrived in London at the head of an F.A. Cup Final special on 5th May 1956, bringing Birmingham City fans to the Capital. The smokebox has been chalked 'Brum 0 Man 5', the correct winners but Manchester City only won 3-1. No 6011 is almost in its final condition carrying a 'WB' boiler with its large superheater cover on the smokebox and double chimney. However, the chimney is one of the narrow fabricated variants, which were less pleasing than the later elliptical ones. Although new to Old Oak Common in May 1928, a move to Bristol Bath Road came in November 1939 but No 6011 was back in London in June 1943. Transferred to Stafford Road in January 1946, it returned to 81A in September 1962 just three months before withdrawal. *RCR5948*

Below: The 5.05pm Paddington to Bristol express passes under Mitre Bridges at Old Oak Common East and is passing over the West London Junction linking the main line with the West London Extension Line to Kensington Olympia, the erstwhile Addison Road station, and Clapham Junction in charge of 81A 'King' No 6012 *King Edward VI* on 8th August 1959. The girder bridge in the foreground carries the WLER on to Willesden Junction's high and low level stations while the bridge behind carries Scrubs Lane, still with its trolleybus wires linking Shepherd's Bush and Harlesden as it would be another three years before routes 630 and 628 were converted to Routemasters. No 6012 was an Old Oak Common 'King' from June 1954, when it moved from Laira, until April 1962 when transferred to Stafford Road. *RCR14072*

Opposite Top: Until the advent of the Type 4 diesel hydraulics the 'Cornish Riviera Express' was one of Old Oak Common's top 'King' workings and the lodging turn was shared with Plymouth Laira with the 81A and 83D 'Kings' alternating the workings of the up and down trains. On 1st December 1957 Laira's No 6021 *King Richard II*, now fitted with a double chimney and four-row superheater boiler, was in charge of the down train, composed of British Railways Mark I stock in Western Region chocolate and cream, and is passing under the flyover bridge at Old Oak Common used by the empty stock workings in and out of Paddington to avoid occupation of the main lines. No 6021 was allocated to Old Oak Common apart from its time at Laira from September 1956 until December 1959. *RCR11431*

Opposite Bottom: With the fireman able to let his fire burn down to avoid excessive blowing off at Paddington, Old Oak Common's 'King' No.6027 *King Richard I* wheels a lengthy up train towards its destination and is seen between Mitre Bridge and the flyover bridge on the approach to Kensal Green Gasworks on 13th August 1960. The leading coach is a strengthening vehicle added to provide extra accommodation and is marshalled ahead of the bogie brake. At this time the 'Kings' were still running high daily mileages and No 6027 would be called into Swindon Works during the following January for what would prove to be its final Heavy General overhaul. Withdrawal would come in September 1962 and like the rest of the class No 6027 remained on toplink duties until condemned, no doubt because of the route restrictions imposed on the class. *RCR15287*

Chapter 3

The 'Castles'

Opposite Top: The 'Castle' class was Collett's enlargement of the Churchward 'Star', although something of a compromise as the use of the new Standard No 7 boiler, as used on the '4700' class, was deemed to be too heavy by the GWR's Civil Engineer's Department. Thanks to the Churchward standardisation principals adhered to in the design, the compromise proved to be a revelation in terms of power and economy. The doyen of the class, No 4073 *Caerphilly Castle*, emerges from the roundhouse at Old Oak Common on 20th May 1956 showing the original design of inside valve cover but carrying a threerow superheater and coupled to the standard Collett 4,000 gallon highsided tender. An Old Oak Common engine from new until July 1950 when moved to Bristol Bath Road, No 4073 was withdrawn from Cardiff Canton in May 1960 after arriving there in January 1957 and set aside for preservation. *RCR5967*

Opposite Bottom: 'Castle' class No 5014 *Goodrich Castle* stands on its home shed of Old Oak Common, PDN is clearly seen behind the front buffer beam, on Sunday, 12th June 1949 in largely unaltered condition, livery apart, since entering traffic during the first week of July 1932. Under the grime is the last version of the GWR's livery, fully lined out midchrome green but with G-crest-W on the tender. The second of the '5013' class that featured modified fireboxes with wider water spaces and a reduced grate area of 29.36sq ft and front valve cover casings with more streamlined fronts. The '5013s' were also given a casing for fire irons on the fireman's side, clearly seen here between the rear and centre coupled wheels. First allocated to Old Oak Common in April 1943, it remained until June 1964 when transferred to Tyseley from where it was withdrawn in February 1965. *John Robertson*

Above: Post-war construction of 'Castles' began in 1946 with Lot 357 for Nos 5098, 5099 and 7000 - 7007 and No 5098 was the first of the class to be fitted with three-row superheaters and mechanical lubricators for the cylinders, valves and regulator. Known as the '5098' class, the second engine of Lot No 357, No 5099 *Compton Castle*, is running light past Old Oak Common East Signal Box on 12th December 1957 and is coupled to Hawksworth flatsided tender No 4121 as it makes its way to Paddington to pick up a down working. The Hawksworth tenders were introduced to the 'Castles' with the construction of No 7008 *Swansea Castle*. Sent new to PDN, No 5099's first move was to Cardiff Canton in May 1948 before being transferred back to 81A in November 1956. Reallocated to Bristol Bath Road in June 1958, it returned to Canton in August 1958 and had spells at Worcester and Gloucester before withdrawal in February 1963. *RCR11323*

Opposite Top: The equipping of the 'Castles' with double chimneys and blastpipes allied to four-row superheater boilers rejuvenated the class as the quality of coal declined. Aesthetically you either hated the look of the front end or liked the modern appearance as displayed by 81A's No 7013 *Bristol Castle* on 21st September 1958, just four months after modification. No 7013 is taking water at one of the two columns close to the shed entrance after having the coal in the tender replenished. *Bristol Castle* is not all that it seems, as it is really No 4082 *Windsor Castle*. The name and numberplates were swapped over at Swindon Works in February 1952 to allow the funeral train of the late King George VI to be hauled by *Windsor Castle* as the original No 4082 was in the works under repair. The subterfuge was necessary as the King, when Duke of York, drove No 4082 at Swindon in 1924. *RCR12771*

Opposite Bottom: Bristol Bath Road allocated No 5057 *Earl Waldegrave* has been serviced and awaits time before returning to Paddington to work back to Bristol on 16th August 1958. Newly fitted with its double chimney and high superheat boiler a month before this photograph was taken, the modified front end exudes power. When released to traffic in July 1936 No 5057 was named *Penrice Castle* but was renamed in October 1937 with the name intended for 'Earl' class 4-4-0 No 3214. First allocated to Old Oak Common in March 1951, it was transferred to Newton Abbot in February 1952, only returning to 81A in March 1960 from where it was withdrawn in March 1964. *RCR12624*

Above: By 1964 and 1965 the last 'Castles' in traffic were in a deplorable external condition as illustrated by No 7008 *Swansea Castle* on its home shed of Old Oak Common on 12th September 1964. Of note is the tender loaded with cobbles of pulverised coal compressed into ovoids that were heartily disliked by footplate crews. The May 1948 built 'Castle' was only transferred to 81A in March 1963, 18 months before withdrawal and had been given its modified draughting and high superheat boiler in June 1959. It seems unlikely that No 7008 has been cleaned since it was prepared as one of the five standby 'Castles' for the Western Region's 'Castle' swansong 'Great Western' special of 9th May 1964 when reckoned to be one of the eight best 'Castles' still in traffic. *RCR17721*

Swindon's allocation of 'Castles' had a number of turns that involved working to and from Paddington and so were often seen in and around Old Oak Common and Scrubs Lane. On 5th September 1955, 82C's No 5068 *Beverston Castle* gets into its stride between Kensal Green Gasworks and Mitre Bridge in charge of the 1.18pm Paddington to Bristol and Weston-super-Mare. Although now five months out of Swindon Works since a Heavy Casual repair in April, *Beverston Castle* is still in sparkling external condition. With a full brake behind the tender the train appears to be made up of a mix of ex-GWR coaches while the empty stock working heading for the carriage sidings features a Hawksworth composite corridor. Released to traffic in June 1938, No 5068 was allocated to Swindon shed from September 1941 until May 1962 when transferred to Oxford from where it was condemned in September of that year. *RCR6627*

It was quite unusual to find double-headed 'Castles' at work in the London area but passing under Mitre Bridge, Old Oak Common East, on 20th August 1955, is an up double-headed express from South Wales as it nears the end of its journey to Paddington headed by Swindon allocated No 7037 *Swindon*, the last of the class to enter traffic, and Gloucester's No 5018 *St Mawes Castle*. Notice that both 'Castles' are coupled to different tenders. The need for a pilot engine is unclear as both appear to be going well and the length of the train is well within the capacity of a single 'Castle'. One likely explanation is that one of the 'Castles' is booked to work an unbalanced turn and this was a way to work it up to London without having to resort to a light engine movement. *RCR6546*

The huge gasworks at Kensal Green, situated between the ex-GWR main line and the Grand Union Canal, dominated the skyline when looking towards Paddington from Scrubs Lane and Mitre Bridge and when the wind was in the east the distinctive smell of the complex was unmistakable. On 13th August 1960, Worcester shed's tired looking No 7002 *Devizes Castle* heads for its home city with one of the regular tightly timed expresses that allowed the 'Castles' to show their fast running capability on Brunel's superbly engineered line to Swindon. No 7002 would be called into Swindon Works for its last Heavy General repair in May 1961. To traffic in June 1946 at Landore, a transfer to Worcester occurred in November 1959. Withdrawal from the cathedral city came in March 1964. *RCR15290*

Above: With less than a month to go before Bristol Bath Road shed was closed to steam after conversion to a diesel depot, the appearance of its top link locomotives was a shadow of what it once was as No 7014 *Caerhays Castle* illustrates on 13th August 1960, heading to Paddington with an up express. The stock also seems to be entirely composed of ex-LMS coaches. Seen approaching the Old Oak Common flyover-bridge, No 7014 was completed in July 1948 and was allocated to Bath Road until September 1960. It then became something of a nomad with spells at Landore, Bristol St Philip's Marsh, Old Oak Common, Wolverhampton Stafford Road, Oxley and Tyseley before withdrawal in February 1965. Given a double chimney in February 1959, it is also fitted with a Davies & Metcalfe lubricator with the oil reservoir mounted prominently on the smokebox. *RCR15288*

Opposite Top: On 29th August 1959, Gloucester shed's 'Castle' No 5017 *The Gloucestershire Regiment 28th 61st* approaches Mitre Bridge in charge of the 2.21pm down parcels ex-Paddington. The immaculate turn out of No 5017 shows the pride of Gloucester shed in 'their' 'Castle', which was renamed on 26th April 1954 after the city's regiment that fought with such distinction in the Korean War. From this angle the double line nameplate and the regimental badge on the splasher are clearly seen. No 5017 entered traffic in July 1932 as *St Donat's Castle* from Taunton before going to Old Oak Common in November 1933. Moving to Laira at the end of December 1934, it was transferred to Worcester in April 1939 where it remained until sent to Gloucester in January 1951. It was withdrawn in September 1962 from Gloucester. *RCR14197*

Opposite Bottom: No 5027 *Farleigh Castle* was in traffic for 28 years and of these 18 were spent at Old Oak Common. However, when photographed at the head of the 5pm Paddington to Bristol express at Mitre Bridge on 7th September 1957 it was at Bristol Bath Road. Unlike the earlier photograph of No 7014 *Caerhays Castle*, No 5027 shows what was Bath Road's normal turn out of its 'Castles'. In the distance an empty carriage working can be seen on the flyover. No 5027 was one of the last dozen 'Castles' to be fitted with a double chimney and blastpipe in 1961 during the engine's last Heavy General overhaul in April. Withdrawal came in November 1962 from Llanelly as the diesel hydraulics took over what had been the principal diagrams of the class. *RCR11204*

Opposite Top: Sir James Milne was the last General Manager of the GWR and in February 1948 it was decided to rename 'Castle' class 4-6-0 No 7001 *Denbigh Castle* in his honour. Introduced into traffic in May 1946 at Cardiff Canton, from April 1948 until August 1961 it was allocated to Old Oak Common. Moved then to Wolverhampton Stafford Road, its last shed was Oxley in September 1963 from where it was condemned during the same month. On 31st August 1957, No 7001, coupled to Hawksworth flatsided tender No 4058, is seen passing under Mitre Bridge in charge of an up express from Weston-Super-Mare and Bristol. During its last Heavy General overhaul in July and August 1960 it was fitted with a four row superheated boiler and double chimney and blastpipe. *RCR11170*

Opposite Bottom: One of Dick Riley's classic photographs of a 'Castle' at speed, epitomising why so many regarded them as one of Swindon's finest designs, shows No 7000 *Viscount Portal* working the down 'Cheltenham Spa Express' at Scrubs Lane on 22nd August 1959 when allocated to Gloucester. The 'Cheltenham Spa Express' title was bestowed on the 8am ex-Cheltenham Spa (St James) and the 4.55pm return working from Paddington and although the train reporting number is displayed in Western Region style it is unusual for the headboard not to be carried at this time. This express was the postwar equivalent of the GWR's 'Cheltenham Flyer', which for many years was regarded as the world's fastest train due to the 67 minute schedule from Swindon to Paddington in 1931. Viscount Portal held the distinction of being the last Chairman of the GWR in 1945. *RCR14187*

Below: The boat train expresses to and from Fishguard were some of the longest diagrammed 'Castle' turns on the Western Region between Cardiff and Paddington. On 1st December 1957, Landore allocated No 4094 *Dynevor Castle*, still relatively unaltered since entering traffic, works an up ex-Fishguard express between Mitre Bridge and the flyover bridge at Scrubs Lane. Recently allocated to Landore, it already shows the attention of the Landore cleaners. Although sent new to Old Oak Common in June 1926, No 4094 was a Laira engine from December 1929 until moved to Canton in November 1937. Apart from between December 1952 to June 1957, when either at Bath Road or Stafford Road, it was a South Wales member of the class at Canton, Landore or Carmarthen until withdrawn in March 1962. *RCR11426*

Chapter 4

The 'Stars'

Below: By 1st January 1948, Old Oak Common no longer had an allocation of Churchward 'Star' class 4-6-0s as they had been superseded by the Collett 'Castles' and 'Kings'. Their transfer away did not necessarily bring withdrawal, rather displacement that reflected the number of new Collett 4-6-0s sent to Old Oak Common. In 1921, the shed was home to 27 'Stars' but a decade later this had fallen to 16. However, this did not stop the class working in from Swindon, Bath Bristol Road, Oxford, Westbury, Newton Abbot and Wolverhampton Stafford Road. On 4th December 1949, Oxford's No 4052 *Princess Beatrice*, in early British Railways livery, has worked up to Paddington and has retired to Old Oak Common for servicing. Behind No 4052's tender is one of the two ash shelters built either side of the coal stage during the war as an air raid precaution and which would be demolished in the 1950s. *Ron Fullagar*

Opposite Top: The 'Stars' were beautifully proportioned and free running locomotives. Even after the loss of their original Churchward 3,500 gallon tenders and turned out in dirty British Railways livery, they looked true thoroughbreds. On 3rd September 1955, Swindon's No 4062 *Malmesbury Abbey* hurries an up express past Old Oak Common East Signal Box before running under Mitre Bridge. Fitted with elbow outside steam pipes, the engine is unusually coupled to a Hawksworth flatsided tender instead of the usual Collett 4,000 gallon type. When Dick Riley took this photograph there were only three 'Stars' still in traffic, Nos 4056 *Princess Margaret,* No 4061 *Glastonbury Abbey* and No 4052. The May 1922 built No 4052 would remain in service until November 1956, leaving the other two in traffic for a few more months. *RCR6624*

Opposite Bottom: A little later in the afternoon of 3rd September 1955, No 4062 *Malmesbury Abbey* runs tender first towards Old Oak Common at Scrubs Lane for turning and servicing. The only steam visible is a wisp over the whistles and the work stained 33-year-old 4-6-0 otherwise appears to be in excellent mechanical condition, although the fireman would have started to allow his fire to burn through well before reaching Old Oak Common East, just three miles from Paddington. The fitting of elbow outside steam pipes indicates that No 4062 has been fitted with new pattern inside cylinders. Interestingly the preserved 'Star' No 4003 *Lode Star* was an Old Oak Common allocated member of the class from introduction through to the 1930s. *RCR6644*

Above: The following year on 20th May 1956, Dick Riley photographed the right-hand nameplate and driving wheel of 'Star' No 4062 *Malmesbury Abbey*. Swindon used a standard backplate with brass beading and each brass letter was attached separately, and on longer names such as this the letters would be placed close to each other. The pre-1914 'Stars' lost the brass beading to the driving wheel splashers and the leading edge of the cab during the Great War, which was never reinstated and so the postwar 'Stars' had this feature omitted from new. No 4062 is in full forward gear and note the difference in wear between the brake blocks on the leading and centre coupled wheel. Also visible is the arrangement of the centre driving wheel springs while the clearance between these wheels and the outside motion brackets is minimal. The fluted connecting rod contrasts with the plain connecting rods. *RCR7281*

Opposite Top: The Talyllyn Railway Preservation Society had requested Bristol Bath Road's last 'Star' No 4056 *Princess Margaret* to work the Paddington to Shrewsbury and return legs of its 1956 Special on Saturday, 22nd September 1956. Thoroughly cleaned for the occasion, the five-coach special was an easy task for No 4056 and its crew. Dick Riley was able to photograph *Princess Margaret* at Old Oak Common the following day before it was worked back to Bristol. According to O. S. Nock No 4056 was held in high regard at Bath Road and was reckoned to be as good if not better than many of the shed's 'Castles'. In the background can be seen one of 81A's three Swindon built Stanier '8Fs' No 48410 while beyond the tender is the shed's breakdown crane. *RCR7998*

Opposite Bottom: On 23rd September 1956, Dick Riley photographed the nameplate and centre coupled wheel of No 4056 *Princess Margaret*, which would prove to be the last of the class to be withdrawn in October 1957. There are a number of interesting differences between this photograph and the similar one of *Malmesbury Abbey*. First No 4056 is in full reverse gear and secondly the driving wheel splashers are riveted to the splasher tops while the brake block wear is much more even. As Princess Margaret had been cleaned for a special working the lining can be clearly seen and No 4056 appears to be fitted with a narrower motion bracket than No 4062. The pipe ahead of the centre-coupled driving wheel is the sand feed. *RCR7997*

Chapter 5
The Pacifics

Below: After an absence of 28 years since the withdrawal of No 111 *The Great Bear* a second Pacific was allocated to Old Oak Common, British Railways Standard 'Britannia' No 70017 *Arrow*, in July 1951, quickly followed by Nos 70015 *Apollo*, 70020 *Mercury,* 70018 *Flying Dutchman* and 70023 *Venus* between August and September 1951. They found little favour at 81A and between December 1956 and February 1957 were transferred to Cardiff Canton where they performed some of their best work on the Western Region. On 9th September 1951, Eric Sawford photographed *Arrow* in front of 81A's repair shop traverser. There was little wrong with the 'Britannias' except for the fact they were different to the shed's allocation of 'Kings' and 'Castles'. *ES220*

Opposite Top: Ten months after arriving at Cardiff Canton shed in September 1952, 'Britannia' No 70028 *Royal Star* was still in immaculate external condition when pictured at Old Oak Common in July 1953 along with a filthy '2884' class 2-8-0 and a 'Hall' class 4-6-0. After working up to Paddington the Canton 'Britannias' were either serviced at Ranelagh Bridge or Old Oak Common, the former when they were working an out and back diagram in a day. After nine years at 86C No 70028 and the other 11 members of the class at Canton were transferred to the LMR as 'Kings' and then diesel hydraulics took over Canton's toplink passenger work. By the time *Royal Star* was condemned in September 1967 from Carlisle Kingmoor it had worked out of Aston (three times), Manchester Longsight (twice), Willesden, Crewe North, Crewe South (twice) and Llandudno Junction.

Opposite Bottom: Cardiff Canton's 'Britannia' No 70027 *Rising Star* is in charge of a Paddington to South Wales express as it accelerates past Scrubs Lane on 12th September 1955. Between 1953 and 1958, No 70027 ran a total of 236,686 miles, most of which were on toplink duties, giving an annual average mileage of 59,172. During this period it underwent two Light Casual repairs at Swindon and a Light Intermediate shopping at Crewe Works. However, when compared to the 'Castles' on similar work there was little significant difference, yet on the Great Eastern Section of the Eastern Region the 'Britannias' ran much higher mileages thanks to the intensive rostering at Stratford and Ipswich and were also regularly recorded running around 90mph on the racing section of line through Diss. After life at Canton *Rising Star* was allocated to Aston, Holyhead, Willesden, Crewe North, Crewe South (twice), Llandudno Junction and Carlisle Kingmoor before withdrawal in July 1967. *RCR6703*

Opposite Top: At Old Oak Common between July 1951 and December 1956 when transferred to Cardiff Canton, No 70020 *Mercury* heads the down 3.55pm Paddington to Cardiff General 'Capitals United Express' past Old Oak Common East on 7th September 1957. The up working was booked to leave Cardiff at 8am with arrival at Paddington due at 10.50am with the locomotive booked to be serviced at Ranelagh Road. Moved to the LMR in September 1961 at Carlisle Kingmoor, between May 1963 and January 1965 *Mercury* was at nearby Willesden where it was one of the shed's best 'Britannias' and used on a number of rail tours including an HCRS trip from King's Cross to York and back featuring some high speeds down Stoke Bank. After spells at both Crewe North and South sheds and both Carlisle Upperby and Kingmoor it was condemned in January 1967. *RCR11198*

Opposite Bottom: Frederick Hawksworth was a lifelong friend of Sir William Stanier and so it is interesting to compare Hawksworth's first GWR design, the 'Modified Hall', with Stanier's first Pacific design, the 'Princess Royal' class. No 46207 *Princess Arthur of Connaught*, one of two members of the class, the other being No 46210 *Lady Patricia*, loaned to the Western Region in February 1956 to cover the temporary withdrawal of the 'King' class 4-6-0s for front bogie examinations and repairs where necessary, is on Old Oak Common on 5th February. Both Pacifics were used on 'King' diagrams in and out of Paddington including the 'Inter-City', 'Cornish Riviera', the 9.10am Paddington to Wolverhampton and some of the Birkenhead expresses as far as the west Midlands. Mechanically the 'Princess Royals' were derived from the 'Kings' and many observers thought that if Collett or Hawksworth had designed a Pacific it would have looked similar to Stanier's first Pacific, albeit with a copper capped chimney and brass safety valve bonnet along with a GWR tender. *RCR5816*

Below: Two Stanier 'Princess Coronation' class Pacifics, No 46254 *City of Stoke-on-Trent* and No 46257 *City of Salford*, were also loaned to the Western Region for three weeks from 28th January to 18th February 1956 to cover the withdrawal of the 'Kings' and during this time No 46257, the last of the class to enter traffic in May 1948, is seen on Old Oak Common. Along with No 46256 *Sir William A. Stanier* F.R.S., No 46257 was built to Ivatt's modified design with foreshortened cab side sheets, rocking grate and Delta trailing truck. These were not the first of the class to be seen at Old Oak Common as No 46236 *City of Bradford* had been used in the 1948 Locomotive Exchanges and from 23rd April to 21st May 1955 No 46237 *City of Bristol* was loaned to the Western Region for trials to see what could be done to improve the steaming of the single chimney 'Kings'. *46257*

Left: Arguably the most unusual Pacific to appear at Old Oak Common was Carlisle Kingmoor's British Railways Standard 'Clan' No 72006 *Clan Mackenzie* on Saturday, 1st December 1963. No 72006 had been booked to work the Home Counties Railway Society's special from Paddington to Swindon and back on Sunday, 8th December and so was coaled and shunted away in the roundhouse by '6100' No 6125. Arriving in grubby external condition, some attempt was made to smarten up the 'Clan' as when it arrived at Paddington a week later it was reasonably presentable. The Sunday was cold and foggy but No 72006 was able to show some of its potential capabilities by some sustained 70mph running on the return trip. The Old Oak management had no intention of keeping No 72006 for longer than necessary and on 15th December packed it off to the Midland Division where it was noted passing through Kettering with an empty milk train. *RCR17447*

Below: The last Pacific to visit Old Oak Common in British Railways days was Stanier 'Princess Coronation' No 46245 *City of London*; carrying a Crewe North (5A) shedplate it is seen here ready to leave 81A for Paddington on 1st September 1964, a little over a week before it was condemned and taken out of service. A Camden (1B) engine from new in June 1943 to September 1963 when moved to nearby Willesden (1A) where it was kept in immaculate condition and regarded as the shed pet. No 46245 was booked to work a return Ian Allan rail tour from Paddington to Crewe via Wolverhampton and Shrewsbury. Injector trouble delayed the departure and the performance of the Pacific was well below what was expected. No 46245's last working was on 13th September in charge of the 5.08am Carlisle to Banbury freight as far as Crewe. *AS Q68-3*

Chapter 6

The Mixed Traffic 4-6-0s
The Collett 'Halls'

The rebuilt 'Saint' No 2925 *Saint Martin*, running as No 4900, is seen at Old Oak Common shed. The PDN on the front valance shows it is at its home depot. It appears to be in British Railways black, and some mixed traffic lining can be seen on the cab side. Coupled to tender No 2253, an intermediate Churchward 3,500 gallon type, no insignia is visible. Technically neither a 'Saint' nor a 'Hall', the engine retained the reversing gear of a 'Saint' and with the lower pitch of the boiler it could not use standard 'Hall' parts as these restricted the use of full reverse. Consequently No 4900 tended to spend longer in the works as parts were sourced. However, as a prototype it proved the concept of the two cylinder 6ft mixed traffic locomotive capable of working all but the fastest expresses and heaviest loose coupled mineral trains. *4900*

Resplendent after its final Heavy General overhaul completed on 18th August 1959, Southall allocated 'Hall' No 4934 *Hindlip Hall* is at Old Oak Common on 29th August. Another of the class with improved draughting, indicated by the X above the cab numberplate, this is the last time No 4934 will appear this pristine, allowing the observer to appreciate the skill of the Swindon painters. Released to traffic in June 1929, *Hindlip Hall* was never allocated to Old Oak Common, although while at Southall from February 1958 until July 1960, when sent to Newton Abbot, it was no stranger to 81A. Withdrawn from traffic in September 1962 from Taunton, after 32 years in traffic it was reckoned to have run over 1.2 million miles in revenue earning service. *RCR14210*

Above: Now sold to a Japanese theme park. the preserved No 4920 *Dumbleton Hall* passes Old Oak Common East Signal Box in charge of a lengthy express for Paddington on 7th September 1957. Allocated to Taunton the boiler carried is one of the higher superheat Standard No 1 design as fitted to the Hawksworth 'Modified Halls' that were interchangeable with the Collett versions but recognisable by the larger lubricator cover on the smokebox. After going new to Old Oak Common No 4920 had three further spells at the shed in the 1930s before moving to Cardiff Canton and then Taunton and Newton Abbot. Its last two years in traffic were nomadic, being allocated to St Philip's Marsh and Barrow Road Bristol before withdrawal from Oxford at the end of Western Region steam in 1965. *RCR11185*

Right: Worcester's longterm resident 'Hall', from December 1941 to December 1960, No 5917 *Westminster Hall* passes under Mitre Bridge and the West London Junction on 7th September 1957 at the head of a down Paddington to Bristol express. Despite its poor external state, No 5917 is obviously in good mechanical and boiler condition as the safety valves are feathering, while there is only the slightest grey haze coming from the chimney showing that, despite accelerating the heavy train, the fireman has his boiler on the mark. A Bristol Bath Road 'Hall' from new in August 1931, No 5917 ended its working life at Southall and was withdrawn in September 1962. In the distance another rake of empty coaches can be seen making their way to Paddington over the flyover bridge. *RCR11186*

Opposite Top: In the 1950s, Oxford regularly had an allocation of around 15 'Halls' and even as late as 1965 the number had only fallen to 11 or 12. Before the introduction of the pressed steel diesel multiple units in the late 1950s, the shed regularly used its 'Halls' on the tightly timed all stations trains to and from Paddington. On 20th August 1955 one of Oxford's members of the class, No 5965 *Woollas Hall*, coupled to an intermediate 3,500gallon tender, makes a fine sight as it accelerates one of the down workings. The usual five-coach set of compartment stock has been strengthened to seven vehicles to accommodate extra passengers. To traffic in June 1938 at Hereford, No 5965 was condemned in July 1962 from Tyseley. During its spell at Oxford No 5965 visited Old Oak's repair shop for a number of unclassified and Light Casual repairs. *RCR6555*

Opposite Bottom: No 6917 *Oldlands Hall* works a long train of empty stock past Scrubs Lane heading towards Old Oak Common East on 3rd September 1955 on the down slow main line. The fireman has obviously built up a good fire and has the safety valves lifting, suggesting that Old Oak carriage sidings may not be the train's destination. The Gloucester 'Hall' has worked up to London earlier and use has been made of it to power what appears to be a fillin turn. The livery is British Railways lined mixed traffic black and no doubt the filthy name and number plates were given a red background when last repainted at Swindon Works in September 1953. No 6917 was allocated to Gloucester from new in August 1941 and remained there until July 1961 when sent to Oxley. Transferred to Banbury in January 1965, it was withdrawn from there in September of that year. *RCR6638*

Above: With their mixed traffic status the 'Halls' were often found working parcels trains and on 8th August 1959 Reading's No 5915 *Trentham Hall* heads for Paddington at Old Oak Common East Signal Box in charge of such a train comprised of the usual mix of ex-GWR Siphons, ex-LMS and British Railways non-passenger bogie stock. In the pre-motorway days of the 1950s the railways were still the fastest means of transporting parcels, post, newspapers and general goods and Paddington was well equipped to handle this profitable business. Trentham Hall entered traffic at Shrewsbury in August 1931 and was a Newton Abbot Division 'Hall' for most of its working life until transferred to Reading in September 1956. It was one of the earlier withdrawals of the class, being condemned during the second week of January 1960. *RCR14075*

On the day it was officially transferred from Carmarthen to Wolverhampton Stafford Road, 13th August 1960, and carrying the correct 84A shedplate, No 4923 *Evenley Hall* works a down vans train under the Old Oak Common flyover bridge. While at Stafford Road No 4923 appears to have been a regular on the West Midlands to London parcels and vans trains. Despite its poor external appearance, the only clean paintwork to be seen is on the cab side where firemen have used the handrail and cab as hand-holds when climbing onto the footplate. No 4923 was not called into Swindon Works for its last Heavy repair until January 1962. Released to traffic in May 1929, No 4923 would not be condemned until May 1964 when allocated to Oxley. *RCR15284*

The main line between Old Oak Common and Paddington was one of the best areas to watch Western Region steam as locomotives from most Divisions regularly worked into the local yards and of course Paddington. At the height of the peak summer holiday season on 20th August 1955, Westbury 'Hall' No 5974 *Wallsworth Hall* heads a down Weymouth express towards Mitre Bridge. Weymouth was not only a holiday resort in its own right but also an important port for ships plying between the south coast and the Channel Islands. When put into traffic in April 1937 No 5974 was allocated to Westbury shed and, apart from a spell at Old Oak Common between October 1941 and July 1944 when briefly sent to Weymouth, it was a long-term Westbury member of the class. Moved to Severn Tunnel Junction in August 1964, it was withdrawn from there in January 1965. *RCR6561*

When painted in British Railways mixed-traffic black lined out in L&NWR style the 'Halls' looked very smart but, unless kept clean, they began to look unkempt and scruffy. On 3rd September 1955 Hereford's No 4905 *Barton Hall*, the fifth of the production 'Halls', looks well turned out, as indeed it should, having only emerged from Swindon Works four months previously after a Heavy General repair. To traffic in January 1929, No 4905 was allocated to Old Oak Common twice, once between November 1932 and June 1934 and again from August 1942 to April 1944. Its last shed was Didcot where it went from St Philip's Marsh at the beginning of November 1963 until withdrawn on the 13th of the month, so whether it ever reached Didcot is a moot point. *RCR6629*

The Mixed Traffic 460s - The Collett 'Hall'

Opposite Top: Another of Reading's allocation of 'Halls' was No 5906 *Lawton Hall* seen on 3rd September 1955 in charge of the 1.10pm Paddington to Chester train as it overtakes an empty coaching stock train on the approach to Mitre Bridge. Again the livery is lined out mixed traffic black with the cycling lion emblem but this is all but invisible beneath the all too usual dirt associated with a hard working steam locomotive. The Hawksworth flat-sided tender No 4109 was coupled to No 5906 from March 1955 until September 1957 and this was the only time Lawton Hall ran with this type of tender. No 5906 only had one short period at 81A between March and August 1952. Put into traffic from St Philip's Marsh in June 1931, withdrawal came in May 1962 from Reading. *RCR6625*

Opposite Bottom: One 'Hall' to go new to Old Oak Common was No 5914 *Ripon Hall* at the beginning of August 1931. Moved to Oxford in October 1931 it was back at PDN in February 1932 but was transferred to Reading again during the following year. On 29th August 1959, it was photographed by Dick Riley in charge of a heavy down relief express to South Wales. In typical Oxley external condition, grime covered and in dire need of a clean, it has worked up to west London from the Birmingham area and been 'borrowed' by 81A to work this summer Saturday extra at a time when Old Oak Common's locomotive resources were stretched. *Ripon Hall* was withdrawn in January 1964 from Gloucester shed having run in excess of 1.2 million miles in service. *RCR14206*

Below: The 'Cambrian Coast Express' was probably Old Oak Common's hardest out and back diagram, as the usual 'Castle' or 'King' was not booked to take coal at Shrewsbury and the train was invariably a heavy one even on the shoulders of the summer peak. On Saturday, 10th September 1960, Wolverhampton Stafford Road's well presented 'Hall' No 6934 *Beachamwell Hall*, complete with headboard, passes under Mitre Bridge in charge of the late running up working, indicating that the 'Castle' or 'King' that powered the down train in the morning had failed en route and No 6934 was Stafford Road's only available pilot. A 'Hall' would have to be in exceptional condition to keep time with this heavy train, let alone one sitting pilot at Wolverhampton. New to Newton Abbot in December 1941, withdrawal came from Banbury in October 1965. *RCR15362*

Westbury 'Hall' No 4933 *Himley Hall* pilots Old Oak Common's 'Castle' No 7020 *Gloucester Castle* working the 6pm Paddington to Weymouth on 8th August 1959, due to connect with an overnight sailing to the Channel Islands. The lengthy boat train was too heavy for either a single 'Hall' or 'Castle' to work to time, an essential with the Channel Island sailings dependent as they were on the tides. If normal Western Region procedure is being followed *Himley Hall* is the booked train engine and *Gloucester Castle* the pilot, in which case it would be interesting to know how the 'Castle' was worked back to 81A. No 4933 entered traffic in June 1929 from Bristol Bath Road and was taken out of service from Shrewsbury in August 1964. *RCR14077*

Chapter 7
The Collett 'Granges'

The Collett 'Granges' were the 5ft 8in 4-6-0s outlined by Churchward in 1901 and long wanted by the Running Department before the introduction of the 'Halls'. They were designed to replace the Churchward '4300' 2-6-0s and incorporated the wheels and motion of the 2-6-0s. The intention was to renew all the 300 or so '4300s' by 'Granges' or the smaller boiler 'Manors' but the programme was abruptly halted in September 1939 with the declaration of war. On 20th May 1964, No 6862 *Derwent Grange* of Oxley shed, coupled to an intermediate tender, emerges from the roundhouse at Old Oak Common. The raised footplate over the cylinders was a helpful feature to identify a 'Grange' along with the lower pitched boiler that gave the class a more robust look. To traffic at Oxley in April 1939, No 6862 was also allocated to Leamington Spa, Oxford and finally Tyseley, from where withdrawal occurred in June 1965. *RCR7275*

This broadside view of Oxley's No 6857 *Tudor Grange* emphasises the more powerful look given by the lower pitched Standard No 1 boiler and 5ft 8in coupled wheels of this 'Grange' fitted with improved draughting, even when in dire need of cleaning. Freshly coaled with some choice lumps of South Wales steam coal, No 6857 is running back towards Paddington to pick up its balancing turn to the West Midlands. The intermediate tender balanced the engine whereas 'Granges' coupled to Collett 4,000 gallon variants always appeared slightly dominated by their tenders. New to Landore in December 1937, No 6857 had spells at Stourbridge, Chester and Oxley before going to Tyseley in May 1965 from where it was withdrawn in the following October. *RCR17510*

Above: Framed by the Old Oak Common coal stage, Pontypool Road's 'Grange' No 6872 *Crawley Grange* displays the early British Railways livery of plain black with the large 'cycling lion' emblem on the tender. Only Nos 6809 *Burghclere Grange* and 6819 *Highnam Grange* received fully lined out mixed traffic black. Pontypool Road 'Granges' were unusual visitors to Old Oak Common but within their red disc route restriction the class were regarded as 'go anywhere locomotives' due to their versatility. No 6872 received lined green livery during a Heavy repair at Swindon in mid-1958. A Truro member of the class until March 1951, when transferred to Pontypool Road, No 6872 was moved to Severn Tunnel Junction in June 1964 and then to Worcester in August 1965, from where it was condemned on New Year's Eve 1965. *RCR6872*

Opposite Top: Five 'Granges' went new to Old Oak Common, including No 6809 *Burghclere Grange*, seen here on 13th August 1960, working hard as it accelerates an eleven coach down express past Kensal Green and the Old Oak flyover. Owing to the lower pitch of the boiler the steam chests were different to those on the 'Halls' and proved to be highly effective, making the 'Granges' very free running up to 70mph and as such many drivers preferred the class to the 'Halls'. Their 5ft 8in coupled wheels also made them able to restart from checks and station calls quickly. Now allocated to St Philip's Marsh, No 6809 is no doubt heading for Bristol. At Old Oak Common between October 1936 and June 1946, No 6809 ended its working life at Southall, from where it was withdrawn in July 1963. *RCR15279*

Opposite Bottom: The 'Granges' were a compact and balanced design and the old adage that if it looks right it is right was never more applicable than when applied to the class. On 10th September 1960, the driver's side of No 6871 *Bourton Grange* is framed by Old Oak Common's coal stage and water tank at the time when it was transferred from Llanelly to Oxley. The March 1939 built 4-6-0 is well turned out considering its last Heavy General repair at Swindon Works was in the summer of 1958 and its red route restriction disc and 'D' power classification above the improved draughting 'X' are all visible along with the orange/black/orange lining. The tender has also been coaled with some choice lumps with no slack visible. No 6871 was taken out of traffic from Oxley in October 1965. *RCR15363*

On Sunday, 23rd June 1957, Bristol St Philip's Marsh allocated 'Grange' No 6842 *Nunhold Grange*, fresh out of Swindon Works after a Heavy General overhaul, epitomises just why so many people held the Great Western Railway and Western Region locomotives in such high regard. The green lined passenger livery is set off by the copper capped chimney, brass safety valve bonnet, brass beading on the driving wheel splashers and the characteristic name and number plates. Stabled alongside a 'Hall' and some 'Castles' it should be noted that GWR 4-6-0s, apart from the 'Counties', did not have front steps so to access the smokebox the usual practice was to use the cab steps and walk along the footplate, although an agile fireman might use the tender steps of a locomotive buffered up, as here, and step across. To traffic in October 1938, No 6842 was condemned in November 1964 from Tyseley. *RCR10812*

Plymouth Laira's 'Grange' No 6849 *Walton Grange* works the 3.18pm Paddington to Wolverhampton express via Oxford at Scrubs Lane on 19th October 1957, as Collett 'Hall' class No 5942 *Doldowlod Hall* works an up van train to Paddington. Apart from the different tenders and the raised footplate over the cylinders on No 6842, it is difficult at this distance to tell the two classes apart. To traffic in October 1937, *Walton Grange* was one of the few members of the class given a Heavy Intermediate repair at Caerphilly Works in March and April 1961 and even more surprising was it being returned to traffic in unlined green. This was rectified in January and February 1964 at Swindon when after its final Heavy General it returned to Oxford shed fully lined out. Withdrawal came from Oxford at the end of December 1965. *RCR11355*

Chapter 8
The Hawksworth 'Modified Halls'

The Hawksworth 'Modified Halls' built by the Western Region, Nos 6981-7929, were all painted black with mixed-traffic lining and entered traffic with Hawksworth flat-sided tenders as illustrated by No 6996 *Blackwell Hall* seen passing Scrubs Lane whilst working an up passenger train to Paddington on 3rd September 1955. Allocated to Taunton at the time, No 6996 had just emerged from Swindon Works after its third Heavy repair the previous April. The tender, No 4062, is the second Hawksworth type to run with No 6996, the first being No 4075, and before No 4062 was attached it had run with three Collett variants. To traffic at Reading at the end of January 1949, *Blackwell Hall* was allocated to Old Oak Common from April 1952 until June 1953 when transferred to Taunton. Withdrawal from Didcot came at the end of December 1963. *RCR10037*

Below: The differences between the 'Modified Halls' and Collett 'Halls' were quite pronounced when viewed approaching, as in this Dick Riley photograph of No 6983 *Otterington Hall* working a Paddington to Didcot five-coach local on 16th August 1958. Having just run under the flyover bridge with Kensal Green Gasworks in the background, an empty carriage working in the charge of a pannier tank can just be seen. The plate-framed front bogie gives the front end a more solid look accentuated by the mainframes extending to the front buffer beam while the long outside steam pipes make the boiler appear to be pitched higher. A '6100' class 2-6-2T would have been easily able to work this train but some of the locomotive diagrams of the period were quite complex and arriving at Paddington with a heavy train, a much lighter working such as this was a way of working a locomotive back to its home shed, in this instance Didcot. *RCR12616*

Opposite Top: After receiving a Heavy General repair at Swindon that was completed at the end of January 1956, No 6974 *Bryngwyn Hall* returned to 81A in immaculate condition and was specially positioned on 20th May for Dick Riley to photograph. Sent new to the shed in May 1950, it remained there until transferred to Southall in December 1961 and was always regarded as one of the shed's better 'Modified Halls' and when ex-works could be entrusted with 'Castle' duties. No 6974 returned to 81A in December 1963 but at the end of February 1964 was sent to Oxford and then Reading before returning to Oxford in November 1964. Withdrawal came in May 1965. *Bryngwyn Hall* was only coupled to a Hawksworth tender twice, when new and from December 1962 until taken out of traffic. *RCR7276*

Opposite Bottom: As befitted one of 81A's best 'Modified Halls', Dick Riley took a fine portrait of No 6997 *Bryn-Ivor Hall* on 20th May standing on one of the ash roads. The front end of the class was different from the standard Churchward/Collett two-cylinder layout. The forged steel extension frames ahead of the outside cylinders were abandoned, replaced by full-length frames. Consequently the cylinders cast integrally with the smokebox saddle and bolted together could not be used so new cylinders and a fabricated smokebox saddle were required along with other frame modifications. Between the frames a fabricated steel stiffener was extended to form the saddle for the smokebox. Within this fabrication were the exhaust pipes from the cylinders to the blastpipe. The front bogie was changed from the Swindon/De Glehn pattern to one with plate frames, a longer wheelbase and individual springs. Inside the Swindon No 1 boiler was a new three-row superheater and a header regulator. *RCR7283*

Above: Four months after Dick Riley took the series of photographs of the newly overhauled No 6974 *Bryngwyn Hall*, he found No 6974 still in immaculate condition as it reversed out of the shed yard at Old Oak Common to make its way light engine to Paddington on 23rd September 1956. This time he photographed the fireman's side showing the Standard No 1 boiler unencumbered with pipework or the footplate with reversing gear. However, there is the fire-iron tunnel coming from the cab to behind the nameplate. The 'Modified Halls' also had longer, less angled outside steam pipes owing to the redesign of the cylinders. The alterations to the front-end included the fabricated smokebox saddle and extended front frames angled down to the buffer beam or plan. *RCR10037*

Opposite Top: Gloucester allocated 'Modified Hall' No 6985 *Parwick Hall* fresh out of Swindon Works after a Heavy General repair and reunited with a Hawksworth tender, No 4122, has just passed Kensal Green Gasworks and the flyover bridge on the approach to Old Oak Common East in charge of a down parcels working on 31st August 1957. The resplendent looking 4-6-0 is passing a steam hauled outer suburban stopping train composed of Western Region red liveried compartment stock. New to Oxley in April 1948, No 6985 was transferred to Old Oak Common the following November before moving to Gloucester in December 1950. After a brief spell at Hereford in 1951 it would remain at Gloucester until withdrawn in September 1964. *RCR11167*

Opposite Bottom: The now preserved No 6989 *Wightwick Hall* of Hereford shed passes Old Oak Common East Signal Box with a local passenger train for Paddington loaded to five compartment coaches on 29th August 1959. Having been in Swindon Works undergoing a Heavy General overhaul in December 1958 and January 1959, it looks as if it hasn't been cleaned since as its once pristine lined green livery has disappeared under layers of coal dust, oil, brake block swarf and general grime. The engine appears to be free of steam leaks but the driver has probably already shut off steam with the fireman allowing the fire to burn down. New to Hereford in March 1948, withdrawal came in June 1964 after spending its working life allocated to Welsh Marches sheds. Sold to Woodham Brothers scrapyard in Barry, it was purchased in 1977 and taken to the Quainton Railway Centre, now the Buckinghamshire Railway Centre. *RCR14199*

Opposite Top: Between September 1953 and June 1965 Didcot shed had between two and five 'Modified Halls' on its books including No 6983 *Otterington Hall* seen here passing Old Oak Common East in charge of the nine coach 5.20pm outer suburban or commuter working from Paddington to Didcot on 8th August 1959. These trains were tightly timed and, when time keeping was poor, the cause of many complaints to Paddington. As with Hereford's No 6989 pictured earlier No 6983 is in desperate need of the attention of the Didcot cleaners, although in three months' time the 'Modified Hall' will be called into Swindon Works for a Heavy Intermediate repair and repaint. To traffic at Old Oak Common in April 1948, it was transferred to Didcot in September 1953 and withdrawn from Oxford in August 1965. *RCR14073*

Opposite Bottom: The penultimate Hawksworth 'Modified Hall' to enter traffic at the end of October 1950, No 7928 *Wolf Hall*, was allocated to Worcester shed all its short working life of just over 14 years, and is seen running light engine to Paddington on the Scrubs Lane empty coaching stock avoiding lines and flyover on 11th April 1964 to pick up its next booked turn to Worcester. Although Worcester kept its last 'Castles' in good external condition, the same cannot be said of *Wolf Hall*. The last two 'Modified Halls', No 7928 and 7929 *Wyke Hall*, were always reckoned to be two of the best of the class yet when withdrawn both had run only a little over 500,000 miles. *Wolf Hall* remained in traffic at Worcester until April 1965 when withdrawn from service. *RCR17499*

Above: Despite closure to steam only now a matter of months away, the interior of the great roundhouse at Old Oak Common was still atmospheric and full of interest, retaining its cathedral of steam aura. On Saturday, 12th September 1964, the sunlight falling through the roof illuminates a work stained but presentable No 6974 *Bryngwyn Hall,* in light steam and now allocated to Oxford shed, as the lined green livery can be made out on both the engine and tender. In the shadows across the turntable are an unidentified '8750' class 0-6-0PT and double chimney '9F' class 2-10-0, No 92237, alongside Southall allocated 'Modified Hall' No 7922 *Salford Hall* and again all three are in light steam. In the foreground can be seen two of the water hydrants used when washing out boilers. *RCR17718*

Photographed along with No 6974 *Bryngwyn Hall* at Old Oak Common shed on 12th September 1964, Southall shed's No 7922 *Salford Hall* presents a more unhappy sight now devoid of nameplates, no doubt stored to prevent them from being stolen. The '9F' class 2-10-0 stabled on the adjacent road is Severn Tunnel Junction's No 92237 and is similarly scruffy but appears to have its safety valves feathering. Also in the photograph is the rear end of Hawksworth '9400' class 0-6-0PT No 9415. No 7922 entered traffic at Chester in November 1950 and was still there in February 1958 when it became part of the London Midland Region but was moved back to the Western Region at Shrewsbury in September of the same year. Moved to Stourbridge in September 1962 and then to Southall three months later, a final transfer to Oxford occurred in August 1965 with withdrawal at the end of the year. *RCR17726*

Chapter 9

The Hawksworth 'Counties'

Below: The Hawksworth 'County' class 4-6-0s were another departure from the Churchward standard two-cylinder parameters. With 6ft 3in coupled wheels, an increased boiler pressure of 280psi, increased superheat and a new design of tender. The boiler made use of the flanging plates designed for the Stanier '8F' 2-8-0s built during the war and the first of the class was fitted with a double chimney. The original plan was to construct 65 examples but only 30 were put into traffic. The doyen of the class, No 1000 *County of Middlesex*, now allocated to Bristol Bath Road, is at Old Oak Common, its first shed, on 5th May 1956, some six months after it emerged from Swindon Works after a Heavy Intermediate repair. Another first for Swindon was the design of the driving wheel splashers. The intention had been to number the 'Counties' as 9900s but when this was leaked to the press the change to Nos 1000-1029 was made. *RCR5944*

Opposite Top: *County of Middlesex* was the only member of the class fitted with a double chimney by the GWR. The remainder were given single chimneys as shown by No 1026 *County of Salop* at Old Oak Common on 9th September 1951. Eight of the class were sent new to Old Oak including No 1021 but by the end of November 1952 all had moved elsewhere. Although given full GWR passenger livery when new, British Railways chose to initially paint the class in mixed-traffic black and under the layers of grime that is the livery of No 1026. In October 1952, *County of Salop* was transferred to Laira but the following March saw it moved to Bristol Bath Road. After a year it was sent to Chester but in September 1955 it was allocated to Shrewsbury from where it was withdrawn in September 1962. *ES228*

Opposite Bottom: The 'Counties' also broke with GWR tradition in respect of their nameplates. Gone were the curved plates over the centre coupled wheel to be replaced by straight plates, similar to those carried by the streamlined 'King' and 'Castle', Nos 6014 and 5005, but with different fittings on the driver's and fireman's side. The driver's side plate was mounted on a separate plate in front of the reversing rod while on the fireman's side it was mounted centrally on top of the splasher as seen here on No 1014 *County of Glamorgan* passing under the flyover bridge with Kensal Green Gasworks behind on 13th August 1960. Fitted with a double chimney in May 1958, the Bristol Bath Road No 1014 is about to start a nomadic life with spells at St Philip's Marsh, Neyland, Shrewsbury and finally Swindon from where withdrawal occurred in April 1964. *RCR15278*

Opposite Top: The driver's side of No 1021 *County of Montgomery* is seen at Old Oak Common during the time the locomotive was allocated to Plymouth Laira (83D), before being fitted with a double chimney in October 1959. As no lining to the livery can be seen it is difficult to say whether No 1021 is in lined black or passenger green. However, as can be seen, the driver's side of a 'County' was quite different from the fireman's side. First there is the ejector pipework partially hidden by the handrail along with the large cover to the lubricator on the smokebox. Second, the unique mounting of the nameplate can be appreciated from this angle as, if it had been placed on top of the splasher, the reversing rod would have partially obscured it. The tenders coupled to the class were wider than the flat-sided Hawksworth type used on 'Castles', 'Halls' and other 4-6-0s. *AEB1965*

Opposite Bottom: No 1012 *County of Denbigh* has its tender topped up at Old Oak Common in August 1954 after being repainted into full passenger livery during a Heavy General at Swindon that was completed on 13th August that year. When seen in this condition the class looked quite magnificent and different from the earlier 'Modified Halls'. Released to traffic in February 1946 at Old Oak Common, it was moved to Plymouth Laira in February 1951. Transferred to Swindon in September 1956, withdrawal came from here in April 1964. When No 1012 emerged from a Heavy General at Swindon in September 1957 its boiler pressure had been reduced to 250psi and the single chimney and blastpipe replaced by the more efficient double arrangement. *NS200633A*

Above: The penultimate 'County' to be built was No 1028 *County of Warwick*, seen here approaching Scrubs Lane in charge of a down express on 13th August 1960, almost at the end of its decade long allocation to Bristol Bath Road shed, after which it moved across the city to St Philip's Marsh. In poor external condition No 1028 seems to be in good fettle and was not called into Swindon Works for what would be its final Heavy repair until February 1962. A Bath member of the class from March 1947, first at Bath Road and then St Philip's Marsh until November 1963 when sent to Swindon. It is doubtful whether it did any work there as withdrawal is recorded as being at the beginning of December of the same year. In its 15 year working life it is estimated to have run almost 724,000 miles. *RCR15280*

Withdrawn on 24th July 1964, Swindon's 'County' No 1013 *County of Dorset* has run up to Paddington and come onto 81A for servicing and appears to be in a cared for condition to the extent that it is hard to believe that in less than a month its fire will be dropped for the last time. However, we are able to appreciate a look at a 'County' in its final Western Region condition carrying lined green livery with the British Railways heraldic device on the tender, the double chimney fitted in February 1958, tender perfectly matching the cab and its front coupling stowed in GWR fashion. New to Bath Road in February 1946, No 1013 also had spells at Laira, Truro and Penzance before going to Shrewsbury in December 1951. A last move to Swindon came in September 1963 from where County of Dorset was condemned at the end of July 1964. *Brian Wadey*

Chapter 10

The LMR & Standard Classes

One of the eight British Railways Standard '5MT' class 4-6-0s loaned to the Western Region in February 1956 to cover the withdrawal of the 'Kings' for urgent frame inspections was Nine Elms No 73110, pictured at Old Oak Common on 4 February. At this time the Western Region had yet to receive an allocation of the class, the first only arriving in March but none in the London Division. By the end of 1957, the region had 35 examples, though still none in the London area. Looking at No 73110's external condition it is hard to realise that it was only new to Nine Elms in October 1955. Arrival at 81A has seen the 70A shedplate removed. As with the Stanier Pacifics on loan the Standard '5MTs' were returned to their home regions as quickly as possible, generally regarded as inferior to the 'Halls'. *LRF2122*

Opposite Top: Standard '5MT' No 73022 arrived at Swindon shed in April 1954 after short spells at Chester (Midland), St Philip's Marsh twice and Landore, where it stayed until September 1958, when transferred to Weymouth. On 12th January 1957, Dick Riley photographed No 73022 passing Old Oak Common East Signal Box in charge of an all stations local comprised of five compartment coaches. At Swindon the '5MT' was placed in the same links as Swindon's 'Halls' which worked to South Wales, Leicester, Oxford and Paddington but was often left as spare. A lot of the antipathy was due to the fact that the Standards were all left hand drive whereas Swindon retained right hand drive and consequently many older drivers found it hard to adjust to sighting signals from the left. No 73022 moved to Eastleigh in September 1964, Guildford in May 1965 and finally to Nine Elms in June 1966 from where it was condemned in April 1967. *RCR11319*

Opposite Bottom: Shrewsbury allocated Standard Caprotti '5MT' class 4-6-0 No 73133 is in charge of the 4.34pm Paddington to Banbury passenger working on 7th September 1957 as it passes Old Oak Common East Signal Box. The Caprotti '5MTs' were rarely seen in the environs of Old Oak Common and Paddington despite the Shrewsbury ten gaining something of a reputation as 'wanderers'. Nos 73125-73134 were usually used on the North-West to South Wales line via Hereford with occasional forays along the North Wales coast during the summer peak period. These Standard Caprotti 4-6-0s were sent new to Shrewsbury between July and October 1956 and all ten were transferred to Patricroft in August 1958 in exchange for the same number of Walschaerts valve gear Standard '5MTs'. No 73133 ended its working life at the Manchester shed in June 1968. *RCR11203*

Above: The junction with the West London Extension Line at Old Oak Common East Junction was an important link to the cross-London route to Clapham Junction and the Southern Region with its Channel coast holiday resorts. In the pre-motorway age the railway was the only realistic link between the Midlands and industrial North for holiday-makers wanting to go to the likes of Brighton, Bognor Regis and Eastbourne. On Saturday, 29th August 1959, Neasden allocated Stanier 'Black Five' class 4-6-0 No 45006 brings a Margate to Derby summer Saturday only working off the junction. Unlike the Collett 'Halls' the 'Black Fives' were allowed over the Southern Region and so were more often than not worked through to the coastal resorts with pilots taken on board at Mitre Junction or Addison Road station. The March 1935 built No 45006 would remain in traffic until September 1967 when withdrawn from Crewe South shed. *RCR14201*

At 11.10am on Saturday, 5th September 1964, Dick Riley captured for posterity this impressive line up of Collett, Stanier and Hawksworth 4-6-0s inside the great roundhouse at Old Oak Common with one of the shed's four undergirder turntables with its boarded top. From left to right are 'Grange' No 6813 *Eastbury Grange* of Worcester, 'Modified Hall' No 6961 *Stedham Hall* of Southall, Stanier 'Black Five' No 44862 of next door neighbour Willesden, 'Hall' No 5933 *Kingsway Hall* of Oxford and Old Oak Common's double chimney 'Castle' No 7032 *Denbigh Castle*. Just what No 44862 is doing on 81A when 1A is just over the Grand Union Canal to the north-west is something of a mystery as the author never saw a 'Black Five' on Old Oak Common shed, let alone one from Willesden, in all the years he visited 81A. *RCR17708*

Chapter 11

The 2-8-0s and 2-10-0s

A panoramic view of Old Oak Common East taken from where the West London Junction provided access to and from the West London Extension Line on Saturday, 7th September 1957, finds no less than six locomotives going about their booked turns. On the up main line is '4700' class 2-8-0 No 4700 in charge of a train from the West Country while on the two lines next to the canal wall, which allow access to and from Paddington without conflicting movements on the busy main lines, finds three 4-6-0s, one '6100' 2-6-2T and a '9700' 0-6-0PT. Much as the Running Department would have liked to use the '4700' class on more passenger work during the summer months they could only be spared on Saturdays when their overnight fast fitted freights did not demand all the class to be in action. Little wonder then that there was little time to clean the big 2-8-0s. *RCR11184*

On Sunday, 19th April 1953, Old Oak Common's plain black '4700' class No 4701 has been coaled and serviced in readiness for its next booked duty. Later No 4701 became the only '4700' to receive lined mixed traffic black. The key to the success of the class was the superb Churchward front end allied to Stephenson's valve gear along with a boiler and firebox that produced all the steam the crew would need, whatever the train. When Churchward retired the Running Department lobbied Collett for more '4700s' but he preferred to build 'Halls', regarding their six-coupled wheelbase as less restrictive than the eight-coupled '4700s' giving the 'Halls' a greater route availability and usefulness. Thought had been given to naming the big 2-8-0s using old Broad Gauge names such as Mammoth, Dreadnought and Behemoth, but as freight locomotives this was not followed up. No 4701 entered traffic in January 1922 and withdrawal came in September 1963. *A R Carpenter*

Above: The Standard No 7 boiler was the largest of Churchward's Standard boilers apart from the one-off fitted to his Pacific No 111 The Great Bear. On Saturday, 11th April 1964, Old Oak Common allocated No 4703 is stabled in the 81A roundhouse alongside two 'Halls', Nos 6937 *Conyngham Hall* and 6947 *Helmingham Hall*, and 'Castle' No 4080 *Powderham Castle* whilst behind is '6100' class 2-6-2T No 6134 with its smokebox door open, a '9700' class pannier tank and another 'Castle'. During their working lives all nine '4700s' were allocated to Old Oak Common/PDN at some time. To traffic in March 1922, No 4703 would be withdrawn in May 1965 and may well have worked its last revenue earning train when photographed by Dick Riley. *RCR17486*

Opposite Top: I was fortunate to see all nine '4700' class 2-8-0s at Old Oak Common or between Dawlish Warren and Dawlish station, but to me their spiritual home was 81A and I regarded them as synonymous with the shed. The series of photographs Dick Riley took of the specially cleaned No 4704 on Sunday, 27th October 1957, helps to explain my admiration of the class. From any angle they were impressive engines with huge boilers albeit with the standard Churchward cab, which had been given extended cab roofs from 1927. In 1932-33 all nine lost their Churchward 3,500 gallon tenders for the Collett 4,000 gallon variant. ATC equipment was fitted between January 1930 and July 1931, the pick-up shoe fitted under the front buffer beam. Completed in April 1922, No 4704 remained in traffic until May 1964 when the last three were taken out of traffic. *RCR11385*

Opposite Bottom: Allocated to PDN at Nationalisation, '4700' 2-8-0 No 4705 was transferred to Plymouth Laira between January 1957 and September 1962 when sent to Southall before returning to Old Oak Common in October 1963 when it was withdrawn. Seen at Old Oak Common on Saturday, 2nd April 1960, along with newly overhauled '8750' class 0-6-0PT No 3688, which would not stay in ex-works condition for much longer. Churchward's use of extension frames bolted to the outside cylinders was a weakness in some of his two-cylinder classes which was ameliorated by the use of stays bolted to the underside of the smokebox and the front framing by the buffer beam. It should be noted that No 4705 does not have snifting valves outside the steam chests as on Nos 4701-4704; instead they are mounted above the platform. The class were also never fitted with steam heat apparatus. *RCR14583*

Having worked a Summer Saturday express up to Paddington, '4700' 2-8-0 No 4706, allocated to St Philip's Marsh, has been used to take empty stock, all British Railways Mark 1 coaches in Western Region chocolate and cream livery, back to the carriage sidings at Old Oak Common to ease congestion and track occupation on the busy Saturday, 16 August 1958. The rake of coaches was probably used Mondays to Fridays on one of the Western Region's named expresses, hence their immaculate appearance. At peak periods 'Kings', 'Castles' and 'Halls' could also be found on similar duties along with freight classes such as the '2800' 2-8-0s. At this time the maximum height at the chimney of the '4700s' was 13ft 4¾in compared to the 12ft 8in of the Mark 1s over the roof mounted periscopes, a feature apparent in this photograph. *RCR12622*

The cab of '4700' class 2-8-0 No 4707 was photographed by Dick Riley at Old Oak Common on Sunday, 16th August 1959. The reversing lever is prominent in full reverse gear, though stabled engines were supposed to be left in mid-gear, while the regulator is mounted in the centre of the backplate. On the driver's side the hydrostatic lubricator favoured by the Great Western can be seen below the driver's brake handle and valve. The gauges on the fireman's side are for the boiler pressure and vacuum brake. One of the water controls for an injector is at the far side with two of the ash pan damper controls. At eye level on the cab side sheet is the caution sign about limited clearances when leaning out of the cab when passing bridges, tunnels, loading gauges and coal stages. Even with the extended roof the protection offered to the crew in inclement weather is rather limited. *RCR14147*

Old Oak Common's work stained '4700' 2-8-0 No 4708 approaches Scrubs Lane and Mitre Bridge in charge of a Paddington to Weston-super-Mare Summer Saturday working on Saturday, 13th August 1960. The last of the class to enter traffic in April 1923, it was condemned in October 1962 along with No 4700. No 4708's last GWR shed was Wolverhampton Stafford Road before being moved to Oxley until October 1952 when allocated to Old Oak Common. As most of the class's revenue earning work was done at night the '4700s' were rarely a priority when it came to cleaning which was a pity as when neglected like No 4708 they really did look awful yet when clean and painted lined green they had an aura matched by few other Swindon classes. Capable of running up to 80mph, the '4700's' cabs carried a plate reminding drivers that the class was not to exceed 60mph. *RCR15299*

In the final days of steam Old Oak Common was used as a dumping ground for many withdrawn classes until individual locomotives could be sold to private scrapyards as Swindon Works did not have the capacity to dismantle the numbers of engines being withdrawn. I remember seeing No 4701 at 81A, seen here on 11th April 1964, with its connecting rods dropped and dumped in the tender but still looking a thoroughbred with the lining on the tender and cab still clearly visible. Alongside No 4701 is an unidentified withdrawn double chimney 'Castle' while further away are a couple of 'Hymek' and 'Western' diesel-hydraulics. Officially withdrawn in September 1963, No 4701 would be sold to Coopers Metals of Sharpness for cutting up on the banks of the River Severn. *RCR17484*

The reduced availability of good quality steam coal after 1945 due to the best coal being exported persuaded the government to sponsor the use of oil firing on the railways. The GWR selected 20 Churchward 2-8-0s for conversion, 12 '2800s' and eight '2884s', all of which were painted plain green and renumbered in the 4800-11 and 4850-57 series. Eleven 'Halls' and five 'Castles' were also converted. The oil tank was placed in the coal space of the tender and was the only outward indication, livery apart, of the conversion. With little or no foreign exchange to pay for the imported oil the experiment was aborted in late 1948 when the locomotives reverted to coal burning with their original numbers. In 1949 No 4857, ex-3831, stands by the oil fuelling tanks at Old Oak Common that were situated close to the canal wall next to an oil-fired 'Castle' or 'Hall'. No 4857 reverted to coal in May 1949 having run as an oil burner for 21 months. *AG227*

That Old Oak Common/PDN was the Western Region and GWR's principal passenger shed did not stop the '2800'/'2884' class 2-8-0 freight locomotives appearing with regularity as they hauled up to West London heavy train loads of Welsh steam coal from the valleys and returned with the empties. On 9th September 1951, it is not a Welsh allocated member of the class seen on shed but Reading's No 2825 alongside 81A allocated British Railways Standard 'Britannia' Pacific No 70017 *Arrow* fresh out of Crewe Works the previous June. As both locomotives are close to the repair shop traverser it is probable that No 2825 requires the attention of the shed's fitters for a job Reading could not carry out. Opposite the coal stage is one of the wartime ash pit shelters erected as an air raid precaution. *ES222*

Opposite Top: At Nationalisation PDN, or Old Oak Common as it had become, had an allocation of 16 '2800'/'2884' class 2-8-0s but in May 1952 the last eight were transferred away. Nevertheless, the class still appeared regularly on shed as they were the Western Region's principal heavy freight class. As well as the almost round the clock movement of coal and empty wagons for the London engine sheds and gasworks such as that at Kensal Green they often worked trains of up to 70 wagon loads of general merchandise. On 23rd September 1956, Severn Tunnel Junction's No 2862, completed in June 1918, has been serviced and coaled with what looks like slack at 81A ready to go back to South Wales. In December 1946 while allocated to Llanelly it was converted to oil-firing and renumbered as No 4802 but in September 1948 reverted to coal firing. Withdrawal came in April 1964. *RCR10043*

Opposite Bottom: Although the Western Region's premier heavy freight class before the arrival of British Railways' Standard '9F' 2-10-0s the Churchward '2800' class were sometimes found on other duties such as here when No 2845 of Ebbw Junction shed was employed on an empty coaching stock train out of Paddington on Saturday, 7th September 1957 passing Old Oak Common East Signal Box. On busy Saturdays it was often a case of using every locomotive that could turn a wheel to keep the traffic moving. Immediately behind No 2845's train is another rake of empty coaches hauled by a bunker first Hawksworth '9400' 0-6-0PT running under caution using permissive block authority. Once the weekend is over No 2845 will return to Newport at the head of a long train of empty coal wagons bound for the valley pits. *RCR11199*

Below: With steam to spare, one of Swindon's small allocation of Churchward '2800' and '2884' class 2-8-0s, No 2890, is making good progress at the head of a down empty stock working out of Paddington on Saturday, 13th August 1960 as it passes Kensal Green Gasworks and the flyover bridge used by many of the empty stock movements. The vacuum braked '2800' class had the same 4ft 7½in diameter driving wheels as the '5700', '8750' and '9400' pannier tanks and were more than capable of accelerating coaching stock up to 35-40mph when necessary. No 2890 was the seventh member of the '2884' class to enter traffic in April 1938 and remained in use until April 1965 when condemned at Ebbw Junction. *RCR15292*

Three of Churchward's 2-8-0s belonging to the '2884' and '2800' classes are stabled on the ash pits at Old Oak Common on the non-passenger side of the coal stage with Cardiff Canton's No 3809 nearest the camera. Behind No 3809 is another '2884' class while the newly ex-works engine at the end is one of the older '2800' class. The '2884' class was Collett's 1938 update of the Churchward design with a side window cab and outside steam pipes. The Churchward design was a remarkably efficient and powerful locomotive, so much so that in the 1948 Locomotive Exchanges No 3803 proved to be as good, if not better, than more modern locomotives, and this with a design dating from 1903. When it was announced that the Western Region was to receive new British Railways Standard '9F' 2-10-0s, the region argued that further '2884' class 2-8-0s would be preferred but to no available. *ES2685*

Between June 1943 and July 1945 Swindon Works built 80 Stanier '8F' class 2-8-0s, LMS Nos 8400-79, that were loaned to the GWR until May 1946 when they were transferred to the LMS to be replaced by 'WD' 2-8-0s. Eight of the class were allocated to PDN where they were put to good use but many drivers disliked the LMS regulator and lack of standard GWR vacuum pumps. After Nationalisation 35 of the Swindon '8Fs' returned to Western Region sheds with three going to Old Oak Common, Nos 48410, 48412 and 48431, between January 1960 and November 1962.

Stabled at 81A No 48431, buffered up to the tender of a '9F' class 2-10-0, shows the modified vacuum ejectors fitted by Swindon in Western Region days with the ejector moved forward on the driver's side of the locomotive to between the two footplate sandbox fillers and Western Region lamp brackets.

Opposite: Southall allocated 'WD' class 2-8-0 No 90355, just out of Crewe Works after a Heavy General overhaul and so still remarkably clean for one of the class, has just brought a train-load of locomotive coal into Old Oak Common on 23rd September 1956 and shunted the wagons into the coal sidings immediately behind No 90355's tender. The imposing façade of the repair shops or factory dominate the background. Built by the NBL Company in September 1944 as WD No 77288, it went to Exeter in March 1947 in exchange for one of the Stanier '8Fs' returned to the LMS. Before arriving at Southall in June 1956 it had spells at Cardiff Canton (twice) and Severn Tunnel Junction before being withdrawn in mid-September 1962. *RCR10040*

Below: Shortly after its naming ceremony at Swindon on 18th March 1960, the last steam locomotive to be built at the works, No 92220 *Evening Star*, is at Old Oak Common on 2nd April alongside '8750' class 0-6-0PT No 8773 and '6100' 2-6-2T No 6115. No 92220 was booked to work its first passenger train on the following day, the LCGB's 'Six Counties' special which it would work from Paddington to Princes Risborough, Oxford and Yarnton. Allocated new to Cardiff Canton, where it was thought the green liveried and copper capped *Evening Star* stood a better chance of being kept clean than anywhere else, it would work a freight down to Cardiff. Canton took a shine to No 92220, regularly booking it to work passenger trains including 'The Red Dragon', until authority took a dim view of the proceedings and reminded the shed that it was a freight locomotive. *RCR14582*

Opposite Top: New to St Philip's Marsh shed in April 1959, '9F' No 92204 is on the goods engine side of the coal stage at Old Oak Common on 2nd April 1960, the same day that Dick Riley photographed *Evening Star*. No 92204 spent the summer of 1960 loaned to Bath Green Park to work the heavy summer holiday trains over the Somerset & Dorset line. The '9Fs' at Bath Green Park were a revelation running over the difficult route, which included the sinuous climb to Masbury Summit, without the need of a banker or pilot. Between November 1960 and April 1963 No 92204 was transferred to 81A before moving to Banbury and Tyseley before seeing out its working life at Speke Junction from August 1966 to December 1967. *RCR8244*

Opposite Bottom: Showing passenger headlamps '9F' No 92212, in typical filthy Banbury condition, powers a down express towards Scrubs Lane on Saturday, 13th August 1960, which, judging from the composition of the train, is a holiday extra. Although authority frowned on the use of the '9Fs' on passenger work the crews took to them like ducks to water. A '9F' invariably rode and steamed beautifully as well as showing a surprisingly good turn of speed. With no speedometer fitted drivers were often surprised to be told just how fast they had been travelling with speeds in excess of 75mph common. No 92212 spent the summer of 1961 at Bath Green Park before going to Ebbw Junction. The following year it was at Tyseley and from there went to Carnforth in October 1966 from where it was withdrawn in January 1968. *RCR15293*

Another '9F' on passenger duty on Saturday, 13th August 1960 was one of Banbury's allocation, No 92214, one of ten of the class at the shed at this time, approaching Kensal Green in charge of an up express. The lack of uniformity in the coaching stock points to this again being a Saturday extra. In the pre-Beeching days rakes of coaches cascaded down from top-link services were retained for the busy holiday periods and this gave the regions the flexibility to put on extra workings when demand was high. No 92214 entered traffic in October 1959 from Banbury, was transferred to Ebbw Junction in December 1961 and after a little under six years was withdrawn from Severn Tunnel Junction in August 1965 almost certainly never having undergone a Heavy General repair. *RCR15277*

Chapter 12
The Smaller Mixed Traffic Classes

Churchward's maid of all work mixed traffic class was the '4300' 2-6-0s introduced in 1911 with the last example completed in April 1932. The class was developed into the '4700' 2-8-0s by Churchward and Collett used parts of the running gear in his 'Grange' and 'Manor' 4-6-0s. Found on both goods and passenger work the Mogul was developed as a tender version of the '3150' class 2-6-2T with an axle loading that allowed a wide route availability. In 1921 PDN had an allocation of 14 engines, a figure that rose to 16 in 1934 and had fallen to 4 at Nationalisation and these were soon moved away. However, the class still continued to appear at Old Oak Common and on 23rd June 1957 Gloucester allocated No 6330, built in April 1921, was photographed by Dick Riley. No 6330 would remain in service until September 1962. *RCR10811*

On 31st August 1957, '4300' class 2-6-0 No 5323 rouses the echoes as it powers its way past Scrubs Lane in charge of the ten-coach 2.35pm Paddington to Devizes and Bristol express. Allocated to Bristol St Philip's Marsh at the time and hauling a train more suited to a 'Hall' or 'Grange', the Mogul appears to have been a last minute substitution for the booked engine, which must have failed. Nevertheless the crew are making a determined effort to run the train to time and the fireman has built up his fire and has the injector on. When worked hard the '4300s' had a reputation of rolling in time to the piston thrusts. Built in September 1917 and fitted with outside steam pipes in September 1946, withdrawal came in June 1958. *RCR1116*

The Collett 'Goods' or '2251' class 0-6-0s was introduced in 1930 to replace the by then long in the tooth Armstrong and Dean 0-6-0s and on 1st January 1948 Old Oak Common had two on its books, Nos 2276 and 2282, to work local goods and pick-up trains. The shed retained a small allocation until 1960 when Nos 2222 and 2276 were transferred away and No 2282 withdrawn. On 31 August 1957 No 2246 of Banbury shed heads a down Class 'K' pick-up goods under the flyover bridge towards Scrubs Lane and Mitre Bridge. With their side window cabs the class quickly acquired the nickname 'Baby Castles'. Built in August 1945, No 2246 was withdrawn in December 1963 from Worcester. *RCR11168.*

'2251' class 0-6-0 No 2222 is pictured in charge of a down Class 'K' pick-up freight passing over the West London Junction and under Mitre Bridge on 12th October 1957. Allocated to Old Oak Common from December 1952 to May 1960, this is just the sort of train the class were built to work and as can be seen the Old Oak cleaners rarely turned their attention to the shed's '2251s'. When transferred to Worcester after the end of its stint at 81A this type of work was being lost to the railways as road transport proved much cheaper and more efficient as loads did not have to be transhipped twice. What work remained could easily be handled by 0-6-0PTs and the by then ubiquitous 350hp diesel electric 0-6-0 shunters. *RCR11328*

Chapter 13

Preserved Locomotives

On 17th April 1960, Old Oak Common was host to Dean/Churchward 'City' class 4-4-0 No 3440 *City of Truro* and Caledonian Railway Single No 123. The pair had been at Swindon for the naming ceremony of British Railways Standard '9F' class 2-10-0 No 92220 *Evening Star*. No 3440 was in charge of the GWR's 'Ocean Mails' special between Plymouth and Bristol on 9th May 1904 and while descending Wellington Bank was claimed to have reached 102mph but this was never authenticated. Whatever speed was attained there is no doubt that it was very high. Withdrawn in 1931 a place was found for it in York Railway Museum where it stayed until 1957 when restored to traffic until 1962. No 123 was built by Neilson & Co in 1886 and took part in the 1888 'Race to the North'. Withdrawn in 1935 she was set aside for preservation and put back into working condition in 1958. *RCR14661A*

When taken out of service in May 1960 the first 'Castle', No 4073 *Caerphilly Castle*, was taken into Swindon Works and restored to as near original condition as was practical given the financial constraints imposed by the British Transport Commission. Once again coupled to a 3,500 gallon tender, the result was a stunning evocation of the GWR in 1923. It was arranged that because of No 4073's importance she would be displayed in the Science Museum in London. Hauled from Swindon to Old Oak Common, Dick Riley was able to take a series of photographs to record the restoration. Here *Caerphilly Castle* has been shunted out of the straight shed into the sunshine of 2nd June 1961. Towed to Paddington by a 350hp 0-6-0DE shunter, she was formally handed over to the Director of the Science Museum before being taken by road to Kensington two days later. No 4073 now resides back at Swindon in the Steam Museum. *RCR115799*

Chapter 14
The '6100' 2-6-2Ts

Opposite Top: The '6100' class 2-6-2Ts were in effect '5101' 2-6-2Ts with the boiler pressure raised to 225psi and introduced in April 1931 to work the Paddington suburban services. In 1950 Old Oak Common had an allocation of 15 '6100' class 2-6-2Ts while Slough had 26, Southall 11, Reading 9, Didcot 5 and Oxford 4. Like all the Swindon large Prairies the '6100s' were handsome, well-proportioned engines that suited green livery, particularly when fully lined out. On 2nd April 1960, No 6163, recently transferred to Old Oak Common from Oxford, is being prepared for its next duty against the backdrop of the shed's repair shop. To traffic in October 1935, it would be condemned from Southall in October 1965. When 81A's outer suburban workings were taken over by the diesel multiple units the '6100s' were successfully used on the empty stock duties in and out of Paddington. *RCR14574*

Opposite Bottom: Slough allocated '6100' No 6133 carrying express headlamps powers a down semi-fast approaching Scrubs Lane on 19th October 1957 while still carrying plain black livery with the large 'cycling lion' totem on the tank sides. The GWR power classification for the class was 'D' blue, which became British Railways '4MT'. With 5ft 8in coupled wheels and a nominal tractive effort of 27,340lbs, the class were sprightly performers with five to seven coach loads such as this one made up of compartment stock used on the outer suburban trains. When introduced the GWR reckoned the class were able to match an 800hp diesel electric in terms of acceleration. To traffic in October 1931, No 6133 was a Slough engine until November 1959 when transferred to Oxford but in January 1960 was sent to Southall from where it was withdrawn in November 1963. *RCR11333*

Below: Until May 1958, No 6145 was a Reading allocated member of the class when moved to Old Oak Common until the shed closed and ended its days at Oxford in December 1965. On a misty Sunday, 1st December 1957 No 6145 is in charge of the 10.12am all-stations Reading to Paddington service as it approaches Kensal Green. The '6100' 2-6-2T was a very successful design that was the final development of the Churchward Large Prairies dating from No 99 built in 1903. Incremental improvements from the first '3100' class through the '5101' class and finally to the '6100' 2-6-2Ts allowed Collett to create the GWR's solution to increasing suburban train loads and sharper timings with most of the '6100s' having a working life of around 30 years, most of which were in the London Division. *RCR11422*

The penultimate member of the '6100' class No 6168, which entered traffic in November 1935, carries express headlamps as it works a down semi-fast past Old Oak Common East Signal Box on 7th September 1957 having just overtaken an empty stock train heading for the carriage sidings. Reorganisation of the Paddington suburban workings in 1955 on a regular interval basis saw some of the '6100s' moved away from the London Division for the first time but it would be the introduction of large numbers of diesel multiple units in 1960 that signalled the end of the '6100s' monopoly on the inner and outer suburban trains such as this one. An Old Oak Common engine for most of its Western Region days, withdrawal came from 81A in March 1962. *RCR11195*

Despite Nos 6100 and 6102 being withdrawn in September and August 1958 respectively, the overhauls of the '6100s' at Swindon continued into 1963 with Nos 6112 and 6167 receiving attention in April. By this date, however, repaints were invariably into plain green as carried here by No 6141 seen at Scrubs Lane on 11th April 1964 when on empty stock duties. As can be seen the class had large lever reversers which did little to ease the rather cramped cabs. Behind the cab footsteps is the substantial balance pipe between the main side tanks and the smaller bunker tank, which between them could hold 2,000 gallons of water while the bunker's capacity was four tons. Apart from the summer of 1960 No 6141 was an Old Oak Common engine until August 1964 when transferred to Southall from where it was condemned in October 1965. *RCR17501*

This panorama taken on 29th August 1959 looking west towards Old Oak Common from over the West London Junction illustrates the extent of the carriage sidings and shed extending way beyond Old Oak Common East Signal Box, the carriage sidings and canal wall but indicated by the plumes of steam rising into the air. Work is also well advanced on the new power signal box, which will replace the GWR built Old Oak Common East box almost opposite. A local up passenger in the charge of '6100' class 2-6-2T No 6127 heads for Paddington. The bridge and steps leading from the towpath on the right was a favourite haunt of spotters and photographers as there always seemed to be something happening. No 6127 was a Slough based engine throughout Western Region steam days and was withdrawn in March 1962 after 31 years in traffic. *RCR14198*

By the beginning of April 1964, Old Oak Common had eleven '6100' 2-6-2Ts still available for traffic while Southall had 18, all of which were in their last months in service and often employed on the empty stock movements in and out of Paddington from the Old Oak Common carriage sidings. On Saturday, 18th April, Southall's No 6139, working bunker first, is in charge of a down empty stock train as an unidentified member of the class heads for the flyover bridge making for Paddington with the stock of a down express. Having spent many hours at Scrubs Lane watching these trains I never saw either a pannier tank or 2-6-2T stall on the flyover whatever the weather or railhead conditions. The November 1932 built No 6139 would be withdrawn during the following November after 32 years in traffic. *RCR17512*

Chapter 15
The Pannier Tanks

After the withdrawal of Dean '1901' class 0-6-0PT No 1912 in December 1949, Old Oak Common was home to five classes of pannier tanks, the Collett '5700', '8750' and '9700' and Hawksworth '9400' and '1500' variants. In April 1955, Eric Sawford photographed three of the five classes together on one of the roundhouse entrance roads: '1500' No 1505, two '5700s', No 8707 and an unidentified engine, and two anonymous '9400s'. The principal difference between the '5700' and '8750' classes was that the latter were provided with improved cabs, 'PJ' boilers, whistle shields and ATC equipment. The new cab incorporated sliding shutters and hinged cab doors. In 1950, no less than 53 of the Collett pannier tanks were on Old Oak Common's books compared with 30 'Castles', 13 'Kings', 25 Collett 'Halls' and 12 Hawksworth 'Modified Halls'. *ES2695*

Pannier tanks by virtue of their relatively low annual mileage were overhauled and repainted less often than top link locomotives such as the 'Kings' and 'Castles' and so many carried their last pre-Nationalisation livery well into British Railways days. On 12th June 1949, Southall's '5700' class 0-6-0PT No 7731 is stabled in front of Old Oak Common's repair shop traverser displaying GWR on its tank sides, allowing an excellent view of the original style of cab. A new piece of plate has been welded into the driver's side tank around the short handrail above the footstep between the leading and centre-coupled wheels. The '5700s' had a distinctive sound when running under light steam created by the vacuum pump. No 7731 was built by the North British Locomotive Company in December 1929 and the builder's plate can be seen on the leading splasher and was withdrawn from Southall in April 1959. *John Robertson*

One of the post-war build of '8750' class pannier tanks was No 9659 that was completed at Swindon in November 1946 and spent all but the last three months of its working life at Old Oak Common. Pictured in as built condition and carrying its only GWR livery of plain black with GWR on the side tanks, it is stabled close to the signal box that controlled the access to the shed. The '5700' and '8750' classes were blue route restriction engines until 1950 when moved into the yellow class, although the condenser fitted Nos 9799-10 remained in the blue group and all were in power group 'C'. Able to negotiate 5 chain radius curves, they could manage 4½ chains at walking pace. After Nationalisation the pannier tanks were rated as '4F'. The first of the classes, Nos 5700 and 5762, were withdrawn in March 1956 and the last, excluding those sold to London Transport, were Nos 4646, 4696 and 9774, condemned in November 1966. 9659 -3752

Above: Built at Swindon in January 1934, '8750' class 0-6-0PT No 8773 was a long-term Old Oak Common resident pannier tank spending its entire Western Region working life at the shed. Seen at 81A on 12th June 1949, it was one of a handful of the class overhauled before British Railways decided on a corporate ownership totem and was turned out carrying BRITISH RAILWAYS in full on the tank sides. It also still carries PDN stencilled on the front footstep in GWR style. Although from No 8770 the new build members of the class were fitted with top feed apparatus, No 8773 carries an older boiler. However, the unidentified pannier tank behind No 8773 does have a top-feed boiler and has the improved cab with its rounded eaves and higher pitch along with larger, more square windows. No 8773 was withdrawn from Old Oak Common in October 1962. *8773*

Opposite Top: The Hawksworth '1500' class was a departure from normal Swindon pannier tank practice, combining austerity with the greatest possible accessibility while reducing the wheelbase to the minimum. Using the non-superheated Standard No 10 boiler the overall weight put the class in the red route classification, which limited their usefulness. Three of the class, Nos 1503, 1504 and 1505, were fully lined out for Old Oak Common's Paddington empty stock duties and when clean looked very smart, as illustrated by No 1505 in c1955, but different. Nos 1500-05 went new to Old Oak Common but Nos 1501 and 1502 respectively were transferred to Southall and Didcot at the end of 1950. Nos 1500, 1503-05 remained at 81A until withdrawn in 1962 and 1963. Nos 1506 and 1507 were also condemned from Old Oak Common having arrived there in May 1962 and April 1960. *NS201272*

Opposite Bottom: The eleven condensing '9700' 0-6-0PTs were built specifically to work over the Metropolitan lines to the GWR's Smithfield Goods depot and all were allocated new to Old Oak Common. No 9710 is seen at 81A on 16th August 1959 and is particularly interesting as it still carries the GWR roundel or 'shirt button' insignia applied by Swindon over 20 years previously. Oddities such as this were hardly unique as five years later 'Manor' class 4-6-0 No 7816 Frilsham Manor turned up at Old Oak Common with a tender still carrying GWR. The Old Oak cleaners seldom turned their attention to the pannier tanks and No 9710 is in everyday condition for the class. No 9710 was released into traffic from Swindon Works in December 1933 and was deemed surplus to requirements in October 1964. *RCR14149*

Below: Another line up of '8750' pannier tanks waiting to come off Old Oak Common on an unrecorded date headed by Nos 8751 and 8771, both carrying top-feed boilers. The engines, however, carry different ownership emblems. No 8751 still has faded GWR while No 8771 has the post-1957 British Railways heraldic crest. The reason for such anomalies was that when a pannier tank was called into a main works for overhaul, if the paintwork was thought to be in good enough condition it was not repainted or simply patch-painted and so retained its existing lettering or crest. Both these engines spent the 1950s at 81A with No 8771 withdrawn from the shed in July 1962 whereas No 8751 was transferred to Newport Ebbw Junction in April 1960 and withdrawn from there in January 1963. *WS2134*

Opposite Top: Old Oak Common's '8750' class 0-6-0PT No 8769 has steam to spare as it passes Scrubs Lane and the former GWR wagon works to the right, in charge of a 'K' class freight on 3rd September 1955. The pannier tanks, rated as '4F' by British Railways, handled much of the heavy local goods work that included working over the West London Extension Line to Kensington Addison Road/Olympia and Clapham Junction and the other cross-London lines to the London Midland and Eastern regions, as well as the empty coaching stock movements between Old Oak Common and Paddington. No 8769 was allocated to PDN at Nationalisation and only moved away in May 1959 when transferred to Southall from where it ended its working life. *RCR6641*

Opposite Bottom: On Sunday, 20th May 1956, two of 81A's Hawksworth '1500' class 0-6-0PTs, Nos 1503 and 1504, are found stabled outside stores and shed office while an unidentified Collett '9300' series '4300' 2-6-0 is on the northern access road to the roundhouse beside the repair shop. The '9300' series, Nos 9300-19, was Collett's update of the Churchward design provided with side-window cabs, screw reverse, outside steam pipes and short safety valve bonnets. At the time Dick Riley photographed the pannier tanks both were carrying mixed traffic lining, the vestiges of which can be seen on No 1503's side tanks. Both worked out of Old Oak Common from new to withdrawal and were credited with 173,745 and 163,673 miles respectively. The highest daily mileage worked by either engine was when sent to Swindon, Caerphilly or Oswestry works for overhaul as in normal traffic they rarely exceeded 50 miles. *RCR5962*

Opposite Top: The condensing pannier tanks, here we see Nos 9700 and 9704 at 81A on 16ᵗʰ August 1959, were as different to the standard Collett design as were the Hawksworth '1500s' and were the first of the panniers to be fitted with the updated cabs. The front of the tanks were foreshortened to permit the large diameter condenser pipes to be fitted and the vertical pipe in front of the dome was the all-important vent. Weir pumps were fitted as when in condensing mode the water in the tanks became too hot for convention cold-water injectors to work. The prominent wheel under the bunker of No 9704 opens a valve that allows the contents of the tanks to be dumped quickly when the water begins to boil after condensing for any length of time. This emptying of the tanks was done at the nearest water column allowing the tanks to be immediately refilled with cold water. *RCR14150*

Opposite Bottom: On a typically grey February day, Sunday 5ᵗʰ 1956, Hawksworth '9400' 0-6-0PT No 9420 has been opened up as it climbs up to the flyover bridging the main lines just west of Kensal Green with a load of nine coaches on the drawbar. This is how countless generations of train spotters who sat on the lineside at Scrubs Lane or stood on the lattice footbridge off the canal towpath remember the up empty stock workings into Paddington, noise, smoke and lifting safety valves. Although not technically one of Dick Riley's best photographs it does convey the drama of a pannier tank making an all out effort. No 9420 was one of the batch built by Robert Stephenson & Co. and entered traffic at Reading in June 1950. Transferred to Old Oak Common in May 1951, it remained at 81A until withdrawn in March 1964. *RCR5811*

Below: The 1.27pm down local from Paddington to Uxbridge accelerates past Kensal Green Gasworks in the charge of Southall allocated '9400' No 9413 on 19 October 1957. Like the '5700' and '8750' classes the '9400's had a fair turn of speed despite their 4ft 7½in driving wheels and were quite at home on inner suburban passenger work. Although capable of working the outer suburban trains, the limiting factor was the 1,300-gallon capacity of their tanks. As can be seen the fireman is quite relaxed having built up his fire before departure time as the safety valves are lifting and the exhaust is clean. No 9413 was another product of Robert Stephenson & Co. and went new to Didcot in March 1950. Transferred to Southall in December 1955, it was taken out of service from there in November 1963. *RCR11339*

Below: '9400' No 9418 heads another train of empty coaches comprised of GWR and British Railways Mark 1 stock onto the flyover bridge between Scrubs Lane and Kensal Green Gasworks as it makes its way to Paddington on 1st December 1957. The plain black livery of No 9418 contrasts with the carmine and cream (blood and custard) of the coaches but with the coaching stock used this intensively was hard to keep clean. I recollect getting heartily fed up of seeing this pannier tank, even though it always appeared to be one of the cleaner members of the class, as it always seemed to be at work during my frequent visits to Scrubs Lane and Old Oak Common. New to 81A in May 1950, the Robert Stephenson built 0-6-0PT was transferred to Southall in March 1965 and withdrawn from there three months later. *RCR11425*

Opposite Top: A busy interlude at Scrubs Lane on Sunday, 1st December 1957, finds a '9400' class pannier tank taking a rake of empty coaches back to the carriage sidings at Old Oak Common and judging from the well wrapped up driver it is a cold day. The coal in No 9418's bunker looks depleted so perhaps the engine and crew are coming to the end of their day's work. More interesting is the empty stock working heading for Paddington with a 'Modified Hall' in charge. If the 4-6-0 is booked to work a down train out of Paddington later it will need to run out to Ranelagh Bridge depot to turn, something that was usually avoided by running tender first, but as this is a Sunday maybe occupation of the line to Ranelagh Bridge will not be a problem. *RCR11407*

Opposite Bottom: On Friday, 21st December 1962, No 9418 has its tanks replenished at Old Oak Common. Under normal circumstances coal would be taken on board once a day but the topping up of the tanks was a constant preoccupation as to run out of water could lead to the dropping of a fusible plug in the firebox with severe consequences. There is little sign of the impending 'Big Freeze' that would hit London on Boxing Day with blizzards bringing chaos to the railways. As can be seen the side tanks were not shaped to fit the boiler, the vertical line from the top small handrail to the support bracket bolted to the running plate marking the inside edge of the tanks. After being in traffic for a while after overhaul, the tank sides of the panniers became stained by the sediments in the hard London water and the water softening chemicals as water was inevitably spilled. *9418*

Chapter 16
The Repair Shop

Old Oak Common's repair shop or factory was to all intents and purposes a mini-Swindon and capable of most repairs except boiler exchanges. Measuring 195ft by 101ft, it housed an electric overhead 30-ton crane supplied by Vaughan & Sons of Manchester and an electric traverser outside that served ten of the eleven roads. The shop was not wide enough to hold engines still coupled to tenders so these had to be separated and left outside. Routine mileage inspections were carried out and whereas some sheds had to rely on shear legs for axle box repairs here, thanks to the overhead crane, they could be completed under cover. In this August 1962 view 'Modified Hall' No 6961 *Stedham Hall* has its front bogie out while the 'King' on the next road is having smokebox repairs. A double chimney 'Castle' and three other locomotives are also receiving attention. With the influx of diesel-hydraulics the repair shop would soon be turned over to their maintenance. *RH178*

Reading allocated '6100' class 2-6-2T No 6104 stands in front of the traverser facing Old Oak Common's repair shop with its rear driving wheels removed to attend to axle box and bearing trouble, probably a hot box. Although the axle boxes and bearings on GWR locomotives were robust and generally trouble free, something as simple as a blocked or fractured oil pipe would be enough to cause overheating and the loss of white-metal and scoring of the journal. The rear axle boxes were of course very close to the ashpan and foundation ring of the firebox and subjected to more extreme temperatures. The Hawksworth flat-sided tender to the right permits a good view of the drawbar coupling, buffers and pipes for the vacuum brake, steam heating and water feed to the injectors. As No 6104 has had its steam heat pipe removed, this photograph must have been taken during the summer timetable. *ES2682*

A rather scruffy 'Britannia', No 70020 *Mercury*, belies the fact that it is still a new locomotive as it waits to enter Old Oak Common's repair shop to have the minor damage caused by a collision on shed put right. The damaged buffer and right hand side of the buffer plank have already been removed along with the drop plate. Even a side swipe at low speed could cause quite a lot of damage and when the boiler pressure was low or the engine was being lit up from cold, the brakes on the engine could be very slow to function and were the cause of many shed collisions. New to 81A at the end of July 1951, it was transferred to Cardiff Canton at the end of December 1956, much to the relief of Old Oak's top-link crews. *ES2687*

Opposite Top: On New Year's Day 1948, Old Oak Common had a single diesel-electric shunter on its books, No 2 (later revised to No 15100), a number that had risen to 18 by November 1963. The GWR took delivery of its first diesel shunter, No 2, in 1936 from Hawthorn Leslie that used an English Electric 6K diesel engine and electric transmission. Allocated to Old Oak Common, No 2 was put to work in Acton Yard. In 1948 Swindon turned out a further six shunters, Nos 15101-106, developed from No 2. The second of these, No 15102, is stabled at Old Oak Common on 9th September 1951 alongside No 13033, a standard British Railways shunter, and an unidentified Swindon shunter. Nos 15101-106 all entered traffic carrying GWR style cast metal numberplates that were later replaced by standard transfers. No 15102 was withdrawn at the beginning of 1968 and cut up at Derby Works. *RCR1274*

Opposite Bottom: In 1934 in collaboration with Hardy Motors Ltd of Southall, the Associated Equipment Company (A.E.C.) and Park Royal Coachworks, the GWR introduced its first streamlined diesel railcar. By April 1936, the GWR fleet numbered 17 cars and included parcels car No 17. The fleet was further expanded between 1937 and 1942 by the addition of 20 Swindon built railcars, the last of which, No 34, was a parcels car, and Nos 35-38 twin-coupled units. The Swindon built batch was easily recognisable by their angular front ends. On 7th September 1957, the Swindon built parcels car No W34W, in maroon livery, passes Old Oak Common East Signal Box working its regular Reading parcels diagram to and from Paddington. Unlike the streamlined cars the Swindon built units were designed to haul a load of up to 60 tons. When No W34W was out of traffic for regular servicing one of Southall's '1400' class 0-4-2Ts would substitute. Entering traffic in September 1941, it was withdrawn in September 1960. *RCR11190*

Above: Carrying carmine and cream livery railcar, No W31W is stabled at Old Oak Common on 21st September 1958. New to Llanelly in February 1941, this car was withdrawn from Southall in August 1962. No W31W's last GWR shed was Worcester and in September 1954 it was transferred to Pontypool Road but during the following month was sent to Southall. The usual work for the railcars in the London Division were services along suburban branch lines, including West Ealing to Greenford and West Drayton to Uxbridge and Staines. Seating capacity was 48. Although not in chocolate and cream livery this British Railways style suited the railcars well enough. The cars looked quite plain and sombre when some were painted in all-over green with cream cat's whiskers on the ends and single cream lining unless newly applied. *RCR12775*

Shortly after the end of the Second World War the GWR started to look at alternatives to steam and initially looked at the gas turbine before going down the hydraulic transmission road. Pre-war Germany had led the development of high-speed diesel engines and hydraulic drives. One of the deciding factors in this choice for the Western Region was the belief that hydraulic transmission was better suited to the South Devon banks. After the cul-de-sac offered by the North British A1A-A1A 'D600' class, a B-B based on the German 'V200' class was adopted and so created the 'Warship' B-Bs. The fifth of the Swindon locomotives built to Lot 428, No D804 *Avenger*, completed in April 1959, powers the down 'Mayflower', the 5.30pm Paddington to Plymouth, under Mitre Bridge and through Old Oak Common East on 8th August 1960. The decision by British Rail to concentrate on diesel-electrics meant No D804 had a short working life and was withdrawn in October 1971. *RCR14074*

The introduction of diesel multiple units on the Paddington inner and outer suburban workings in 1959 reduced the available work for the '6100' class 2-6-2Ts and in 1959 and 1960 Old Oak Common lost 11 of its allocation and those that were left were reduced to stand-by duties to cover failures of the diesel multiple units or working the empty carriage duties to and from Paddington. Typical of the duties undertaken by the three-car sets is this Paddington to Oxford service nearing Scrubs Lane on 2nd April 1960 comprised of two sets. The big advantage of these units over the '6100s' was their ability to work intensive diagrams whereas the 2-6-2Ts needed to keep their water tanks filled and go on shed for coal and routine servicing. *H36-4*

The arrival of the first three 'Western' class C-C hydraulics caused something of a stir at Old Oak Common due to their eye-catching styling and liveries. If No D1000 *Western Enterprise* in desert sand livery caused people to stop and stare in disbelief, No 1001 *Western Pathfinder* in maroon with yellow buffer beams was quite breathtaking as when seen here at 81A in February 1962. On the other hand No D1002 *Western Explorer* in green with yellow buffer beams was less different from the 'Warships'. The 'Westerns', however, marked the rapid demise of the 'Kings' and accelerated the withdrawal rate of the 'Castles', including the double chimney rebuilds only recently given a new lease of life. Although the 'Westerns' soon lost their ex-works finish, the sound of their twin Maybach MD655 engines as they accelerated heavy South Wales expresses through Scrubs Lane always left a lasting impression. *D1001*

Above: The introduction of the Blue Pullmans onto the Western Region in 1959-1960 brought a vivid splash of colour to Old Oak Common where the region's three sets were based. Few who saw the Pullmans when new will forget the impression they made with their streamlined power cars and stunning Nanking blue and white livery. The Western Region sets were used on the 'South Wales Pullman', the 'Birmingham Pullman' and the 'Bristol Pullman'. On 12th September 1963, one of the Western Region eight-car sets stands outside the new straight diesel/Pullman shed at Old Oak Common with DMBS (driving motor brake second) No 60094 nearest the camera. As well as losing their Pullman crests, when given full yellow warning panels the driving cars seemed to be less different. When the livery was revised to grey instead of Nanking blue with dark blue window panels this again did nothing for the aesthetics of the Pullmans as the new paint quickly weathered. *AS O30-4*

Below: The collaboration between the British Transport Commission Design Panel and design consultants Wilkes & Ashmore of Horsham came up with a very good looking locomotive in the Beyer, Peacock built Type 3 'Hymek' B-B diesel hydraulic. The stylish design was augmented by the use of a two-tone green livery with off-white window frames. Unlike the 'Western' class the 'Hymeks' had a single Maybach engine and Mekydro transmissions and were equally at home powering 12-coach expresses or branch line pick-up freights and were intended to replace the 'Hall' and 'Grange' 4-6-0s. Introduced in January 1961, from February 1962 small yellow warning panels were carried from new. On 11th April 1964, 'Hall' class No 6937 *Conyngham Hall* is seen at Scrubs Lane hauling two 'Hymeks', Nos D7059 and D7064, towards Old Oak Common. Both Nos D7059 and D7064 were withdrawn in October 1971. *RCR17502*

As Old Oak Common's allocation of '6100' 2-6-2T and pannier tanks was withdrawn, a suitable diesel replacement was sought for the empty stock movements to and from Paddington. The Swindon built 'D6300' class B-B hydraulics that had first been used in Devon and Cornwall but had later spread over most of the Western Region south of Birmingham were drafted in from 1964 until withdrawn between 1967 and 1972. The relatively non-demanding nature of this work saw the annual mileages of the 'D6300s' drop markedly. On 18th April 1964, newly overhauled No D6326 hauls a rake of empty coaches out of the sidings at Old Oak Common and is about to pass under the footbridge leading off from the canal towpath. Released to traffic in May 1960, withdrawal came at the beginning of October 1971 after just over 11 years in service for an estimated cost of £64,500. *D6326*

Chapter 18
The End of Steam at 81A

Below: The steam shed at Old Oak Common was deemed to be unsuitable for housing the growing fleet of diesel-hydraulics and diesel-electrics and in 1964 a start was made in demolishing the buildings. However, as the last steam locomotives were not made redundant until March 1965 it could not be razed in one fell sweep. On 11th April 1964, the two eastern turntables were cut up and the roof and supporting walls over them removed leaving the entrance façade still standing. In this view a 'Hymek' can be seen stabled alongside one of the western turntables. Boiler wash-outs were still carried out at the far end of the shed but most locomotives still rostered for work were stabled alongside the coal stage. *RCR17480*

Opposite: By 12th September 1964, Old Oak Common had just three 'Castles' left on its books, Nos 7008 *Swansea Castle*, 7029 *Clun Castle* and 7032 *Denbigh Castle* and one of these, No 7029, is stabled out of steam inside the roundhouse building. With little or no work left for the class No 7029 was transferred to Gloucester during the first week of October 1964 where it worked goods and parcels traffic along with special passenger trains. When withdrawn it was bought for preservation by Patrick Whitehouse and based at Tyseley. After the shed closed to steam the remaining buildings, along with the coal stage, were demolished but one turntable was retained, along with its wooden boarding and stabling roads, for use by the shed's diesels. *RCR17719*

Dick Riley took a number of photographs of the partially demolished shed at Old Oak Common on 11ᵗʰ April 1964, and in this one the turntable pit can be seen after the cutting up of the turntable. Stabled under the remaining sections of roof are a 'Warship' diesel-hydraulic B-B, a departmental coach that was either part of the breakdown crane train or a mess coach, a '6100' 2-6-2T and a pannier tank. That the remaining structure looks secure and safe is thanks to the strength of the original design. However, by this date the remains of Old Oak Common shed were no place for casual visitors. The shed closed almost 59 years to the day since it opened and thanks to the likes of Dick Riley we still have a most comprehensive record of the shed's heyday and inevitable decline. *RCR17485*